Peace in the Puzzle:

Becoming Your Intended Self

Peace in the Puzzle: Becoming Your Intended Self

Susan Myhre Hayes

myhre hayes GROUP LLC
Minneapolis

This book draws on the experiences of the author. When appropriate, the thoughts of other authors are cited either in the text or at the end of this book. Most of the names used as examples have been changed although the thoughts and ideas remain true. Those that shared the letters to their younger self agreed that their words could be used in this book and other writings by the author when identified by their initials, the year of their birth and their gender. Some identifiers were changed at the request of the submitter.

PEACE IN THE PUZZLE: BECOMING YOUR INTENDED SELF Copyright 2011 Susan Myhre Hayes. All rights reserved. Printed in the United States of America. No part of this book may be used or reproduced in any manner whatsoever without written permission except in the case of brief quotations embodied in critical articles and reviews. For information, www.peaceinthepuzzle.com

First Edition

Book and cover design by Elisabeth J. Hayes

ISBN 978-0-578-078-19-9

Peace in the Puzzle: Becoming Your Intended Self © Susan Myhre Hayes

For Oliver & Eloise —

Whom I visualize will find and achieve their pieces of the puzzle much sooner than I, in part because of my love and this book.

Acknowledgements

Many people spent time and energy to make this book a reality. Each brought their love for me and their unique talents to the effort, and I acknowledge and thank each of them for their contribution.

To Mary Carroll Murphy and Julie Stroud, who were gentle, consistent and effective editors.

To Tom Eckstein, who as requested regularly asked about my progress towards completion.

To my early readers – Lou Burdick, Sue Hinkin, Jill Jetter, Barbara Lupient, Kathleen Riley, Chris Roberts and Monica Schultz – your insights and reactions were vital parts of the process.

To Elisabeth Hayes, who captured the spirit of the book in the beautiful jacket and in the formatting of the text and was an early and lasting cheerleader for the project.

To Carolyn Adams, who ensured that all citations gave credit where credit was due – correctly.

To Eric Hayes, David Nash and Betty and Jim Myhre, who were a vital part of my journey to this book.

To all those, who generously shared their advice to their younger selves and became voices of wisdom some whom I know and others whom I will never meet.

To my husband, Greg Hayes, who knows sometimes better than I do who I would be without his steadfast and enduring love.

Table of Contents

Introduction	*1*
How to use this book	*4*
Chapter One	
The Puzzle, My Piece of the Puzzle and Other Puzzle Pieces	*7*
Chapter Two	
GPS: Tools for Your Journey	*18*
Chapter Three	
Advice from the Voices of Wisdom	*23*
Chapter Four	
Your Invitation to the Prom: What You'll Need to Attend	*30*
Chapter Five	
Looking Back: Your Tracks in the Snow	*37*
Chapter Six	
The Power of Thought: Your Subconscious Mind	*49*
Chapter Seven	
The Power of Thought: Affirmations	*58*
Chapter Eight	
The Power of Thought: Personal Talking Points	*66*
Chapter Nine	
The Power of People: Together We Are an Ocean	*81*
Chapter Ten	
Harness the Power of People: Your Personal Board of Directors	*109*
Chapter Eleven	
Snap: Four Steps to Self-Transformation	*118*
Chapter Twelve	
Get to "just do it": Motivation	*135*
Chapter Thirteen	
Harness your Resources: Needs and Wants	*155*
Chapter Fourteen	
You are Unique in the Universe:	
Consider All Sources as You Look for Repeating Lessons	*174*

Chapter Fifteen
    Reprogram Self-Sabotage: Road Blocks   **188**

Chapter Sixteen
    The End of My Year and the Beginning of Yours   **202**

Deep Dive Workbook
    Chapter One: Deep Dive   212

    Chapter Two: Deep Dive   215

    Chapter Three: Deep Dive   216

    Chapter Four: Deep Dive   217

    Chapter Five: Deep Dive   218

    Chapter Six: Deep Dive   220

    Chapter Seven: Deep Dive   222

    Chapter Eight: Deep Dive   224

    Chapter Nine: Deep Dive: Friends   226

        Deep Dive: Family   227

        Deep Dive: Marriage and Partnerships   228

        Deep Dive: Overall Relationships   229

    Chapter Ten: Deep Dive   231

    Chapter Eleven: Deep Dive   233

    Chapter Twelve: Deep Dive   236

    Chapter Thirteen: Resources: Deep Dive   238

        Job: Deep Dive   243

    Chapter Fourteen: Deep Dive   248

    Chapter Fifteen: Deep Dive   254

    Chapter Sixteen: Deep Dive   259

Appendix
    I.   Personal Talking Points   263

    II. Affirmations   266

    III. Your Personal Talking Points   270

    IV. Your Advice to Your Younger Self   271

    V. Your Tracks in the Snow   272

    VI. Parking Lot   273

    VII. References   274

Introduction

I have always been writing a book of some kind. I started each with lots of energy but never finished them. To add to the embarrassment, while I was not aware of this pattern, others were.

A clarifying moment came one New Year's Eve. When my children were young, I began an annual New Year's Eve tradition, and my son's friend, David, was always included. We made predictions for each other and for ourselves for the coming year. After dinner, we reviewed the predictions from the previous year and enjoyed their varying degrees of accuracy. Then, each of us wrote and read aloud our predictions for the upcoming year. We tucked them away until the next New Year's Eve when the process started again. This particular year, before we started writing our predictions, David said to everyone, "No one – including Susan – gets to write that Susan will finish her book this year. We write that every year, it never happens, and we need something new."

No malice, just a statement of fact.

Anyone who knows me knows that I am a completer; a get 'er done kind of person. So, why was writing a book something I could not complete?

This is a story I was born to tell, but it is story I could only tell after 60 years of living. My true goal had always been to share the story of my 59th and 60th year, my years of transformation, to help others transform themselves just as I did. The book was merely the vehicle.

During these two transformational years, I realized that each of us is part of something larger, something I liken to a jigsaw puzzle. Each of us has a unique role to play in this puzzle, reinforced by each of us being born at a unique point in time. Each of us has a unique piece of the puzzle. The desire to fulfill our unique role tugs at each of us much like a small child tugging at our sleeve in order to get our attention. We are incomplete until we understand and perform the unique role we are to play; the puzzle is incomplete when we are not fulfilling that role.

During these two transformational years, I discovered my true goal was not just to write any book but to find and fulfill my unique role and write a book about the process. My piece of the puzzle is to help others find theirs. I write this book to inspire others to find their own true greatness; to help others find their piece of the puzzle and thereby their peace in the puzzle.

During these two transformational years, I took what philosopher Soren Kierkegaard called a "leap of faith". But, as he said, "Leap of faith – yes, but only after reflection."

Sixty years of reflection to be exact.

My puzzle piece includes telling the story of these two transformational years, sharing the tools I used along the way so that you can find your puzzle piece. My purpose had always been to tell this story so you have a sense of confidence and optimism as you transform and transcend to claim your piece of the puzzle. As you transform to become your intended self. As you find, claim and perform your unique role.

When I realized this, I felt a contentment I had never felt previously. I had found my piece of the puzzle. And by so doing I found my peace in the puzzle.

I tell this story to help you find yours.

This book isn't about me. It is about you.

How to Use this Book

This is not a how-to-book. It is a "how-I-did-it-and-how-you-can-too-book." It is my hope that you can use the story of my transformation to my intended self as a model for how you can do the same. In each chapter, I will tell you some of the relevant parts of my story, share the tools I used and continue to use to be who I was always intended to be.

It is also a how-I-did-it-and-how-you-can-too-*workbook,* and you may want to write as you read. Start by putting the date you begin reading this book on the inside cover. Later this will help you mark your progress on your journey. The side margins going forward are wider than most books, so that you can write your ideas as you read. The end of every section is an opportunity for reflection on what you learned called Notes to Self. Use it to write your thoughts about the chapter, no matter how incomplete they are. At the end of the book is a "deep dive" section for each chapter with questions to prompt you to think about the content of each chapter and what it means for you. Honor how the book and workbook will best support your work. As you begin, I suggest that you suspend judgment and be curious about this material and your reactions to it. Write often and freely.

As with all things, ultimately, your attitude will determine how you use this material and the results you get. As you approach ideas that may be new to you, I suggest that you be:

- Comfortable with a skeptical attitude as to whether this will work or not. Give it your best shot anyway.
- Non-judgmental as to whether the information provided is good or bad. Try it whether you believe it or not.
- Comfortable with the pace at which things happen and with being the expert in your own life.
- Mindful that you are aiming to become something you already are. Trust your own wisdom.

To get a reality check on my ideas, I asked several of my friends to read initial drafts of this book. Besides encouraging me to publish the book, each of them "did" the book differently. I give you permission to do the same. One started writing her personal talking points as soon as she read chapter eight and didn't get back to chapter nine for several weeks. Another was so enamored with the voices of wisdom in chapter three that she spent some time writing what she would say to her younger self right after reading it. I was encouraged by the engagement that my words produced in them, but I suggested to them – as I do now to you – that you read the entire book before you begin your work in earnest.

Once you have read all the chapters and have the whole picture, I suggest that you review your notes, make more notes and begin to make your plan using the deep dive section. That said, as with all things, there is no *right way* to utilize this book. I urge you to make the process of how you use it your own as you find your way to your intended self.

Bon Voyage!

Chapter One

The Puzzle, My Piece of the Puzzle and Other Puzzle Pieces

Once upon a time, there was a farmer who raised wonderful corn. Every year he entered his corn in the state fair, and every year he won the blue ribbon. One year a reporter interviewed him and asked the secret to his success.

"My secret is that every year I share my seed corn with my neighbors," replied the farmer simply.

"How can you share your best seed corn with your neighbors when you know they are entering corn in competition with you each year?" the confused reporter asked.

"You have to understand how corn growing works," said the farmer. *"The wind picks up pollen from the ripening corn and blows it from field to field. If my neighbors' corn is inferior, cross-pollination will steadily degrade the quality of my corn. If I want to grow good corn, I must help my neighbors grow good corn, too."*

Just like this farmer who saw a bigger view than just his own farm, I see the universe as a big jigsaw puzzle. I am part of this puzzle, one unique piece of it, as is everyone, including you. I imagine what the puzzle looks like without my piece and then I imagine what it looks like with my piece in place. It feels right and complete.

My commitment to transform began when I knew three things: I was an integral part of the puzzle; I had a unique role to play in the puzzle; and I was not fulfilling my unique role.

Sometimes I call this something larger the cooperative universe. Other times I call it a puzzle, a corn field or the God of our understanding. The name is not important. Nor is it important whether I am religious or not, attend church or not, consider myself spiritual or not. I know with confidence that I am a part of something bigger than myself. Something in aggregate larger than any of us alone. And there is something I am assigned to do; something I am intended to do.

The cooperative universe provides each of us with exactly what we need to grow on our journey to find and claim our place in the puzzle. These lessons are, however, often presented in unexpected ways, so each of us needs to be open to special deliveries. The two lessons that finally brought the purpose of this book into focus came in just such an unanticipated way.

The first was my decision to get a tattoo. I did not know much about tattoos having been raised in a family who believed they were the domain of drunken sailors on leave in a foreign port. So I learned from my daughter the importance of the symbol you choose for a tattoo. My daughter juggled a successful modeling career with school work during both high school and college. It was often difficult. When she graduated from college, she marked the occasion by getting a tattoo of a sprig of rosemary. Rosemary from Italy where she lived and worked, rosemary to remind her of the wonderful smell from the bushes in front of her grandparent's house in Arizona, rosemary which represents steadfastness, and rosemary that grows better in adverse conditions. A perfect choice. A perfect way to mark her occasion.

On my 59th birthday, I decided to get a tattoo on my 60th. It is an easy decision to get a tattoo; it is more difficult deciding what it should be.

I spent the better part of the year thinking about the literal shape my tattoo would take. During this time, I began to carefully examine the course of my life, unconsciously and haphazardly looking for my tracks in the snow and my personal talking points. To know how I would literally mark myself, I needed to understand what was important to me.

My tattoo is a symbol from Ghana that stands for self-transformation. After looking for nearly a year, the cooperative universe led me to this symbol. When it did, I felt peaceful. I felt confident. I had no doubt. I admire people who self-transform and began to believe that I could do the same. The symbol is on my lower back and on every page of this book.

The second lesson from an unexpected source came from Ralph, the man who cleans my house. One day, we were chatting about both being 60 years old. He said, "I don't know about you, but I always thought that some day I would wake up and find out I was doing something completely different, and that my life was not what it is today. That never happened. Too late now, I guess."

Most of us have had such moments of clarity when we realize we are off-track somehow. Ralph's statement was just such a moment for me for this was the moment this book came into focus. I recognized my piece of the puzzle. It was not the book itself that was important; it was the *content* of the book. I was to be the voice that helps others find their intended selves, just like Ralph helped me. By finding my piece of the puzzle, I was to help others find theirs to complete the puzzle. I knew I would do whatever it took to intentionally transform to fulfill my role.

Many times in my life, I gave in to the currently popular phase, "*It is what it is.*" In my 60th year, I decided "it" (the role I was to play as my destined self) was not *what it is* because *it* was not yet what it was intended to be. I decided I could close the gap between the life I was living and the life I wanted to live, the life I was intended to live. It was within my control to make it "*what it is.*" Not only could I claim my piece of the puzzle, but that each of us could claim our unique position in the universe and play the role we were meant to play, no matter our age or circumstance. And, I could supply the tools I had used to do just that.

In my 60th year, I did what it took to transform to the person I was intended to be all along. I quit drinking alcohol, got my finances under control and let go of expectations I had of others. I finally wrote this book.

Ancient Greek philosophers believed that nothing comes from nothing. They believed that what exists now has always existed, and that nothing new could come into existence unless there was something before. The flip side of this was that nothing could be destroyed.

If nothing comes from nothing, and nothing can be destroyed, then there is a finite amount of material in the puzzle that is continually recycled, material that endures. Everything – including us – is part of this continually recycled material.

And, while every particle of this material can change form, it does not change its essence. Every single part of this recycled material has a purpose – a unique, enduring place in the world. Each of us, being a unique configuration of this material with our own essence, is meant to find and claim our place in the puzzle. We all yearn for the journey that will lead us to find our one-of-a-kind piece and, thereby, the role we were meant to play, the person we were intended to be, the person we know in our mind's eye, the person we long to discover and be.

And, we love stories about people who have done just that.

The Harry Potter story is one such example. Harry, after years of sadness, torment and a feeling of not belonging, is rescued from his Aunt's house where he lives in a space under the stairs. This rescue begins his journey, and he discovers that he is actually a wizard and a hero. It is a journey to his birthright. Suddenly, Harry goes from living a life of unhappiness to living a life with a very unique purpose - a purpose vital not only to Harry, but to the well-being of the entire wizard world as well.

Harry's story may be the most popular at the moment, but some form of Harry's story has fascinated humans for centuries. Luke Skywalker, Princess Leia, Frodo, King Arthur, Odysseus and a host of other fictional characters were all on a journey to understand who they were and what part they would play in the world. A journey to find their puzzle piece. A journey to become their destined self.

We love these stories because each of us is on a journey of our own. And just like each of these fictional characters, we long to be the hero of our own story by finding our place in the universe; our piece in the puzzle.

If this longing in life is unfulfilled, the tension between our life as it is and our life as it should be leads to feelings of sadness and depression. According to work done at the Centers for Disease Control, one in 20 Americans aged 12 and older are unhappy and depressed[i]. Much of this unhappiness and depression may be the result of the discrepancy between the life we are currently living and the longed for life with a purpose that is uniquely ours.

I felt this tension most of my adult life. But during my 59th and 60th year, I learned how to become the hero of my own story. I decided to transform – intentionally. I claimed my birth right.

I decided what I wanted to create in my life, and what I needed to change utilizing tools I had found throughout my journey. Those tools helped to create a self-fulfilling prophecy.

You are reading this book because, on some level, you are hoping to find and claim your piece of the puzzle and thus find peace and contentment in the same way I have. I want to help you become the hero of your own story. I write this book in the hopes you can find and claim your essential, authentic puzzle piece sooner than I did. Consider each chapter to be a guidepost for your journey and use the *Notes to Self* space that follows to chronicle your thoughts. Deep Dive Exercises for each section are available at the end of the book when you are ready to immerse yourself in the material and ideas presented.

While I want you to find your authentic, only-yours puzzle piece for your own sake, I also want you to find it for the sake of us all. I believe we are all a part of something larger than ourselves. I call the force that is larger than all of us the cooperative universe; others call it the God of our understanding. You will find your own name for this force. I visualize the cooperative universe as a jigsaw puzzle, and to be complete every puzzle piece needs to be in place, with each of us performing our role. Each of us needs to be our intended self. One only need read a newspaper to know that the universe urgently needs your contribution. It will – as it always has – support you in finding it.

I can say it no better than the German poet, Johann Wolfgang von Goethe:

> Until one is committed, there is hesitancy, the chance to draw back, always ineffectiveness. Concerning all acts of initiative and creation, there is one elementary truth, the ignorance of which kills countless ideas and splendid plans: that the moment one definitely commits oneself, then providence moves as well. All sorts of things occur to help one that would never otherwise

have occurred. A whole stream of events issues from the decision, raising in one's favor all manner of unforeseen incidents and meetings and material assistance, which no man could have dreamed would have come his way. Whatever you do, or dream you can, begin it. Boldness has genius, power and magic in it. Begin it now.

If you have ever felt the tension between the life you are living and the life you are intended to live, continue reading. If you are longing for something more in your life, use my story and the tools I used as a guide. If you have ever felt yourself a part of something larger, don't hesitate. Don't draw back. Commit yourself to the journey to take your place in it.

Begin it now.

Once you believe that Goethe's providence —or what I call the puzzle or the cooperative universe —will support you in unimagined ways, you will find your puzzle piece – the *unique* role that you will play in the puzzle. And once you find it, you will begin to live the life given to you alone. When you find your piece in the puzzle, you will find fulfillment and contentment. You will find your peace in the puzzle.

S.M.H 1949 ♀ 른

Notes to Self for Chapter One

Want to work on the ideas in this chapter further? Deep Dive Exercises for Chapter One are on Page 212.

Chapter Two
GPS: Tools for Your Journey

Once upon a bright and sunny day, a woman was sitting in her car. She had a longing to go somewhere but wasn't at all sure where that was or how to get started on the journey. She sat in the car and pondered for many days.

One day, she got an inkling that she was meant to drive to the ocean. She'd always been drawn to the ocean but had never seen one. So she started the car and put the car in gear, only to realize she couldn't see through the windshield. Eventually, she discovered the windshield wipers and with a clean windshield, she was on her way to the ocean.

As she started on her way, she discovered that with bright sun in her eyes, she couldn't navigate. She stopped. While it took her awhile to find a store where she could purchase the right pair of sunglasses, she did, and she was on her way to the ocean once again.

Then she noticed a flashing light on her dashboard.

She stopped, consulted the owner's manual and learned that the problem indicated by the light could be addressed within the next 2,000 miles. So, with a clean windshield, good sunglasses and the confidence that she could wait on the needed repairs, she was once again was on her way to the ocean.

The flashing light on the dashboard kept distracting her. She looked at it so frequently that she missed several of the turns that would take her to the ocean.

She decided to stop and get the needed repairs.

So, with a clean windshield, good sunglasses and no more flashing lights, she was on her way to the ocean once again.

To get to the ocean - telling the story of my transformation in this book - I had to be able to drive my car. To do that, I needed to clean the dirty windshield (stop drinking alcohol) so I could clearly see the path. To clearly see the path, I needed to get a pair of sunglasses (let go of expectations of others) so I wasn't blinded by the sun. To clearly see my path, I needed to repair my car (take control of my finances) so I was not distracted. Until then, not only was I not able to see where I was going, I wasn't even sure which ocean I wanted to reach. Once I was driving, my GPS gave me options as to which ocean I wanted to find. I used the tools in following chapters like a GPS. I used it to find my piece of the puzzle, my intended self.

The cooperative universe supports us in unimagined ways, and the tools I used are provided by the cooperative universe. I will share how they worked for me and how they might work for you. While I cannot tell you where your journey will lead you, consider this book the GPS for your journey to find and claim your unique piece of the puzzle.

I invite you to use my story and the tools I used to support your journey to claim your puzzle piece and discover the person you were meant to be. The tools will ask you to:

- Imagine something larger than yourself that wants to help you.
- Look backwards to find your tracks in the snow.
- Open yourself up to the possibilities.
- Consider the power of unconventional thinking.
- Look for patterns.
- Utilize the power of thought.
- Establish a personal board of directors.
- Find and use your turning points.
- Understand your motivation.
- Harness the power of the puzzle.
- Reflect on the influence of others in your life.
- Think about the resources available to you.
- See yourself as unique.
- Make notes to yourself though out this process.

As you begin to use these tools, know that there are many ways to get from here to there. As with everything, you get to choose. The GPS merely provides a suggested route. Stray from the route, and the GPS will recalculate. Turn off the GPS for awhile and it will begin to provide direction from wherever you are, whenever you need it again. The GPS provides options. The choice is yours.

Ready to turn on your GPS?

Notes to Self for Chapter Two

Want to work on the ideas in this chapter further? Deep Dive Exercises for Chapter Two are on Page 215.

Chapter Three
Advice from the Voices of Wisdom

t one of my college reunions, ten of my closest college friends came from all over the country to stay in the dorm, reconnect and reminisce. It was wonderful.

At the college I attended, reunions took place during the same weekend as graduation. I remember clearly when the ten of us were walking down a long flight of outdoor stairs just as we saw the line of fresh faced graduates in their gowns beginning to walk up the same stairs. As if on cue, we all stepped aside and let them pass.

As they passed, I asked my friends, "Do you think we should tell them?"

After a long silence, one of my friends replied, "They'd never believe us."

I'm not sure what I meant by the comment nor am I sure what we would have told them, but in hindsight, I think my friend was right. They never would have believed us.

In my 58th year, still seeking material for the ever elusive book I had failed to complete, I sent the following note to everyone I knew:

Subject line: Your advice requested

Thanks to the magic of email, you are receiving this email via a friend, who may have received it from a friend of a friend of a friend, and so on.

This request originates from Susan Hayes located in Minnesota, USA. Susan is collecting advice. She wants advice from you. To celebrate what you have learned on your journey and to share those lessons with others in a book she hopes to write, this is an invitation to give your advice in the form of a letter to your younger self.

Here's what to do:

1. Pick a point in time when you were younger. You may pick the day you graduated, the day you got your first job, the day your heart was broken for the first time, or you may just want to divide your current age by two.

S.M.H 1949 ♀ 듬

> 2. Write a letter to your younger self and provide the best advice you can give. This is your letter, and there are no rules, but to help your thinking, the letter could give advice as business-like as "plastics" ala 1970's movie with Dustin Hoffman, The Graduate, as practical as "only floss the teeth you want to keep," as meaningful as "have confidence in your intuition," as spiritual as "open yourself up to the universe and the universe will provide every thing you need" or a combination of all of these. What do you wish you would have known?
>
> 3. To protect your confidentiality, please provide the following as an identifier - first and middle initial and your year of birth followed by an ♂ if you are male and an ♀ if you are female – at the beginning of your letter, i.e. B.W. 1959 ♀
>
> 4. Share this invitation with as many of your friends as you like and ask them to do the same.
>
> Returning the letter will indicate that your responses can be used anonymously in full or partially in a compilation of this research in a book or report format.
>
> Thanks so much for helping to share what you have learned!

I set up an email address to receive the information, and not only did I receive wonderful advice, I also got some suggestions on how to get more letters to a younger self. Some people asked if they could raise the question at a family gathering and report the results. With my blessing, they did just that. Some people suggested that I go to Senior Centers and ask the residents what advice they would give to a younger self. I did just that many times, and I believe that they enjoyed the group conversations almost as much as I did.

So throughout this book, you will see "Voices of Wisdom" that contain gems of advice to a younger self gathered via email, snail mail, family gatherings, book club discussions and Senior Center gatherings. It should be noted that except for spelling corrections, I did no editing of these submissions. Likewise, some of the advice contradicts other advice given in the book, and I have made no attempt to remedy the discrepancies. They point to the unique aspects of each of us. It is my hope that you will find the messages provided by these voices of wisdom interesting, provocative and heartwarming. I hope they will make you think about what advice you would give your younger self, and in the process, understand that now is always the perfect time to follow that sage advice.

In sharing the letters to their younger self with me, each agreed to let me use their words in this book using their initials, the year of their birth and their gender as an identifier. Some of the Voices of Wisdom writers asked that their initials be changed as they thought there close association with me would make their comments recognizable to some. I have honored their wishes. Here is one of my favorites

> I wish that I could have believed, like Dorothy, that I had everything inside me all along. I'm finally just beginning to understand how fully capable and powerful I really am. To begin to live life freely, without that nagging self inside of me keeping me down, is joyous.
>
> V.A. 1924 ♀

I now believe, like VA and Dorothy in the *Wizard of Oz*, that I had everything inside me all along. I had everything I needed to live the life I was always meant to live. I always had the truth of my life's purpose within me, but never recognized it. Only I knew with certainty that I had an important piece of the puzzle. Only when I heard Ralph's story and read the words of the Voices of Wisdom, only then did I begin to recognize it as truth. Ask yourself what it would take for you to listen to truth while you read the following story.

Once upon a time Truth walked the streets completely naked looking for people who wanted to enter into a discussion. Because he was naked, no one wanted to talk to him. When people caught sight of him, they turned away and fled.

One day when Truth was wandering around, he came upon Parable, who was dressed in splendid clothes of beautiful colors. Seeing Truth, Parable said, "Tell me, friend, what makes you look so sad?"

Truth replied sadly, "Ah brother, things are bad. I'm very old, and while I have Truth, no one will speak to me. I am sad because they will not know Truth."

Parable said, "People don't run away from you because you're old, Truth, for I too am old, and the older I get, the better people like me. Because I too want people to know Truth, I will tell you my secret: People like things more when they are prettied up and disguised. Let me lend you some of my splendid clothes of beautiful colors, and you will see that the same people who ran from you yesterday will invite you into their homes today, be glad of your company and listen to you."

Truth took Parable's advice, and somewhat disguised when dressed in splendid clothes of beautiful colors, people did listen to Truth. From that time on, Truth and Parable have always gone hand in hand.

I have always had the truth of my purpose within me. One some level, I knew what my puzzle piece was and what I was intended to do as my life's purpose. So do you.

S.M.H 1949 ♀ ䷁

Notes to Self for Chapter Three

Want to work on the ideas in this chapter further? Deep Dive Exercises for Chapter Three are on Page 216.

Chapter Four

Your Invitation to the Prom: What You'll Need to Attend

A young woman complained to her grandmother about her awful life. She told her how hard things were for her, how she did not know how she was going to make it and how she wanted to give up. She was tired of struggling. It seemed as one problem was solved, a new one would take its place.

Her grandmother took her to the kitchen. She filled three pots with water and placed each on a fire with a high flame. When the pots came to a boil, she placed carrots in the first, eggs in the second and in the last pot she placed ground coffee beans. She sat in silence with her granddaughter watching the boiling pots for twenty *minutes. She turned off the burners, took the carrots out and placed them in a bowl, took the eggs out and placed them in a bowl, and ladled the coffee into a third bowl.*

She asked her granddaughter what she saw.

Only carrots, eggs, and coffee, she replied.

Her grandmother asked her to feel the carrots, and the young woman discovered that the carrots were soft.

The grandmother asked her to take an egg and break it, and the young woman found a hard boiled egg.

Finally, the grandmother asked her granddaughter to sip the coffee. The granddaughter smiled because the coffee was just as she liked it.

Questioningly, the granddaughter looked at her grandmother.

Her grandmother explained that the carrots, the eggs and the coffee had all faced the same adversity — boiling water — but each reacted differently. The carrot went in strong, hard, and unrelenting. After being subjected to the boiling water, it softened and became weak. The egg had been fragile, with just a thin outer shell protecting its liquid interior. When it encountered the boiling water it hardened.

However, the ground coffee beans were different. When they encountered the boiling water, they transformed the water.

Over the years, I have been many Susans. I have most likely been a carrot, an egg and a coffee bean, for I have been the Susan people wanted me to be. I've been the Susan I *thought* people wanted me to me. I've been the Susan who was as perfect as possible because I was an extension of someone else. I have been the secret Susan. I've been the Susan I became without even knowing it.

> My advice to you at that young age would have been to let go of expectations about being in charge or in control.
>
> D.S. 1949♀

It took me nearly 60 years to find the Susan I was born to be, the Susan that embodies my essential nature — the authentic Susan. The Susan I was intended to be to complete my piece of the puzzle. Once I glimpsed the authentic Susan, I became her easily and amazingly quickly. It was easy because I had been getting nudges in the direction of this essential Susan all my life. I realized I had been close my whole life.

I have made a myriad of choices and lived in a myriad of circumstances. Some of these choices I knowingly made, while others I made not realizing I was making them. Some circumstances, like the family I was born into, were thrust upon me, while others, like the jobs I have performed, have been within my control. I posed the *advice question* because I was frequently lost in the *what ifs* of my journey. What if I had taken physics instead of physiology in high school? What if I had chosen another college to attend? What if I had not married so young? What if I had continued teaching? What if I never had children? What if I could have given my younger self advice? The list of *what ifs* was long.

On some level, I felt there was a life I was meant to be living; a role I was destined to play in the world. There was a person I was intended to be. And I was not living the life I was intended to because of my choices and my circumstances.

If only. What if?

Deadly words.

My father once told me a story of an overweight high school girl named Joanie. Joanie dreamed of going to her high school prom. She knew exactly the dress and shoes she would wear and the hairdo she would create. In her mind's eye, she could see herself there.

She was, however, never invited to the prom and was convinced she was not invited because she was overweight. Joanie was saddened by this fact but did nothing to lose weight. Perhaps she feared if she did lose weight, she still might not be invited. She liked knowing that she wasn't invited because of her weight. She liked the certainty that going or not going to the prom was in her control. It was her weight that was holding her back, yet she never took control of her weight.

Over thirty years ago, I wrote in my journal that I had just realized the steering wheel for my life was directly in front of me, and I only needed to reach out and take the wheel. I now know this feeling is called *self-efficacy* – the belief in one's ability to accomplish a task by one's own efforts. It was a powerful feeling. It was a new feeling for me. It was also a fleeting feeling for me. Like Joanie, I saw the wonderful things I could do, yet I did nothing to reach out and take the wheel in front of me.

> The world you see is the world you've seen. So, get out there have new experiences.
>
> M.H. 1955 ♂

Thirty years later, my hands are on the wheel, and I am no longer a prisoner of the *what ifs*. I have self-efficacy. I believe in my own power to impact my life, and each day I am much closer to the role for which I was born.

S.M.H 1949 ♀ 🗏

Your journey is of your own making no matter what your choices have been or your circumstances may be. The cooperative universe urgently longs to have you find your puzzle piece and will support you in unimagined ways to do just that. Just as you long to discover your puzzle piece, the cooperative universe longs for a completed puzzle.

> You will be bombarded by messages from many sources. Pay attention to the ones that make you ponder.
>
> R.K. 1939 ♂

I invite you to continuing reading, suspend judgment, be curious about yourself and your reactions to this material, write in the margins, write notes to yourself at the end of the chapter, decide when to work on the deep dive exercises at the book and eventually develop your own program for your transformation. Whether you are 25 or 65, beginning a career or retiring and starting an encore career, refocusing your direction or lost in possibilities, this is the beginning of your transformation to your intended self.

This is your invitation to the prom. This is your invitation to discover and claim your puzzle piece.

Everything you need to attend will be provided in the following chapters.

Welcome to the prom.

Peace in the Puzzle: Becoming Your Intended Self

Notes to Self for Chapter Four

Want to work on the ideas in this chapter further? Deep Dive Exercises for Chapter Four are on Page 217.

Chapter Five
Looking Back: Your Tracks in the Snow

O nce upon a time at a large university, the president, being a woman of order, was concerned about the fact the students did not walk on the sidewalks. This resulted in sad looking grass, and additional maintenance costs associated with continually making that sad grass look happy again.

Announcements were made to get the students to stay on the sidewalks, speeches were delivered, emails and texts were sent to get the students to stay on the sidewalks. They still walked on the grass.

Frustrated, the President consulted with a motivational specialist before the school year began in the fall. After hearing about the problem and touring the campus, the motivational specialist assured her that for $10,000, he could get the students to stay on the sidewalk.

She was delighted.

School started, and the students continued to ignore the sidewalks. The President continued to be upset. The motivational specialist did nothing.

The leaves began to fall, the students continued to ignore the sidewalks. The president continued to be upset. The motivational specialist continued to do nothing.

By Thanksgiving, the President had had enough and angrily called the motivational specialist.

"When are you going to do something?" she demanded.

"Patience," he said, "I will have an answer for you by year's end at the latest, and a solution for you by spring."

> I wish you could look back from where I am. Some things seem less important than they were, and some seem more important than I made them out to be. If something keeps coming up, you might want to pay attention to it sooner rather than later.
>
> B.B. 1933 ♂

By spring, the motivational specialist had contracted with a landscape architect to take out the old sidewalks and replace them with new ones. And, lo and behold, the students stayed on the sidewalks.

The President happily paid the bill for $10,000 but called the motivation specialist out of curiosity.

"How did you get the students to walk on the sidewalks?" she asked.

"After the first snowfall, I took pictures of where the footprints were and put the new sidewalks where the students were already walking."

In the story above, the path was always there. The students were on their path. The sidewalks were in the wrong place and someone else's idea of where the path should be. Finding the path took looking at how students moved through the campus by noting their tracks in the snow.

As children, we all dreamed of what we would be when we grew up. This was true for me. At the age of six and long before her famous nephew George was born, I dreamed of being singer Rosemary Clooney. I would sing her songs while standing on a chair in an effort to be a more grown-up size. Even at the age of six, I had a vision – albeit a foggy one – of the person I was meant to be. Even at a young age, my tracks in the snow were leading to my piece of the puzzle.

Years later an astrologer told me when she reviewed my astrological chart for me she assumed I was a singer because it indicated that I was born for my voice, I thought of myself standing on that chair.

> Consider what the poet, Robert Brault said, "Looking back you realize that a very special person passed briefly through your life, and it was you. It is not too late to find that person again." Then go looking.
>
> J.J. 1948 ♂

Only in the last few years have I seen clearly that the voice she saw as an essential part of me was not the singing kind of voice but rather the voice of a spokesperson. Only in the last few years have I found that voice first for myself and then as an advocate for others finding their own voice. Finding and claiming their puzzle piece just as I have.

What do you see when you look back?

The universe wants each of us to find our piece of the puzzle and supports us in so doing. The universe tugs at our sleeves to get our attention. The universe provides tools, and we need only harness them.

Your first tool requires you to have 20/20 hindsight. This isn't hard, for things do seem clearer looking backward than they do looking forward. Hindsight is the ability to turn around and see your tracks in the snow.

In the same way, on the journey that is your life, on your journey to find who you were meant to be, you will need to rediscover your footprints. No fear, the footprints are there. Remember, you were born to be on this journey and the cooperative universe provides exactly what you need to get there. Perhaps, at the time, you just weren't paying enough attention to the valuable information the footprints reveal.

My tracks in the snow indicate that the universe was always directing me to write. My tracks in the snow show me that sharing my journey would help others on theirs. I am the person who was meant to write this book.

First, my tracks in the snow pointed to writing:

- My mother, a stay-at-home mom who had previously worked in a job requiring extensive writing, used to sit with me at the kitchen table and talk me through my writing homework. I had this personal writing coach for most of my life.
- I always loved books and was an English and German Literature major in college.
- My Masters degree was in teaching composition, and research in that area at the time pointed to

> No knowledge is wasted —you will use it some day in some fashion. Respect the value of education — and the lessons gained through experience—in all their forms. It is amazing how everything ... all the education, all the life experiences, all the peaks and valleys that come from life's joys and sorrows ... all seem to make sense and fall into place in one's brain, just as much of the rest of one's body is falling apart.
>
> J.D. 1949♀

the unique nature of every person's writing process. Through my studies, I came to see the rumination process that preceded my writing as part of my writing process. I began to see myself as a writer.

- Every job I have ever had has required me to write, even though writing was not listed in the job description.
- In my 40's, a woman I consider to be a very good writer told me I was a terrific writer, and she knew she'd be reading a book of mine someday.
- For the past 30 years, I have been writing books. Ask anyone who knows me, and they'll probably say, "That Susan. Always working on the book but never completing it." Once Ralph's comment pulled my thoughts into focus, I went back and collected nearly 30 years of incomplete writing projects and folded them into this completed book.

Second, the "sharing my journey beginning with this book" tracks in the snow:

- I was always intrigued by the question, "If you knew then what you know now, would you do it differently?"
- Before this book came into focus, I sent letters requesting people share what advice they would give to a younger self.

> Music is in your blood. Don't deny it. You never had a choice about what you were going to do. It is and always was your gift. Music.
>
> **G.A. 1947♀**

- I worked for several years at a nonprofit that helped "displaced homemakers" find their way back into the work force following divorce. This was during the '70s and at the beginning of the women's movement, so many of these women were unprepared to take care of themselves. While they had the mink coat and diamond jewelry, they had no marketable skills. I will never forget the women who came to our offices each day. I was often called on to talk about how I got back into the workforce after taking time off when my kids were small.
- In my 30's, an attorney with whom I was working told me I had a unique perspective on people and a unique way of saying things. "Ever think of a book?" he asked.
- At a time when I was working three jobs to make ends meet, I was trained to teach parenting classes to parents of children with learning disabilities. The focus of the classes was teaching self-efficacy to children. At the end of each class, parents often thanked me for helping them find their way as a parent.
- In my 50's, an astrologer told me she thought I was a professional singer because she got a strong indication of voice, and my voice would make me famous. While I have been in many choirs and love to sing I have never been ac-

cused of being a lovely singer. I now see that the voice she sensed had to do with my finding my own voice and helping others to find theirs.

- Since I was small, people I know well and those I hardly knew have easily confided their hopes and dreams to me. Most said they felt better following the conversation.

- One of my guinea pig readers whom I have known since kindergarten said, "My image of your gift was your *speaking* voice – your ability to think quickly on your feet, in a charming and inquisitive manner, fed by your quick wit and wide base of knowledge base." Hearing that another friend said, "And you know how to gently help people."

> Watch less television and more life.
>
> E.B. 1934♀

In each of these tracks in the snow, the cooperative universe was providing me exactly what I needed on my journey to writing to help others find their piece of the puzzle. Nudging me in the direction of my intended self. My mother's coaching was an unlikely gift from a woman who otherwise had little time for me. I like to think her teaching me the structure of writing was part of her gift and part of her puzzle piece. All of my educational pursuits and my ever changing career path have directed me towards writing. My need to write was an indication that I should write. The encouragement to write from mere acquaintances was clearly a nudge. If I had been open to it, the message from the astrologer could have told me I might find my voice through my writing. But, I didn't see it. I only saw these tracks looking backward.

Some people call these "God nudges".

Some people call them trusting your gut.

Some people call them dumb luck.

Some people call them opportunities.

Some people call them signs.

Some people call them the answer to prayer.

Some people call then the unique path given you at the time of your birth.

Whatever you call them, know that you have them. Know that by looking at your tracks in the snow, you can discover where the cooperative universe has been directing you. And, if you don't believe you do, act as if you do. The rest will follow.

Look for your tracks in the snow. Look for patterns in your life. Look for the nudges the cooperative universe is giving you every day. If you are having trouble getting started, people who knew you when you were younger are a good resource, as are friends you have known for a long time.

> Think about when you are old. What will you have to tell your grandchildren about your grand journey? What stories will you have to tell? Will they be the ones you want to tell?
>
> R.W. 1940 ♂

So while you have been on this journey your whole life, you can now consciously examine what those tracks in the snow mean for your choices going forward. Be curious about what their pattern means and where they are leading you.

I often think of the movie *City Slickers*. Curly, the surly cowboy played by Jack Palance, has the following conversation with city slicker Mitch, played by Billy Crystal.

> Curly: You know what the secret of life is?
> Mitch: No, what?
> Curly: This. (He holds up his index finger.)
> Mitch: Your finger?
> Curly: One thing. Just one thing. You stick to that and everything else don't mean shit.
> Mitch: That's great, but what's the one thing?
> Curly: That's what you've got to figure out.

Your *one thing* is what makes up your puzzle piece, and your tracks in the snow have been leading you to find it. Your tracks in the snow are there to lead you to discover the unique role that your intended self is destined to play.

Want to know the color, shape and texture of your puzzle piece? To paraphrase the famous modern philosopher, Curly, you've got to figure that out.

Peace in the Puzzle: Becoming Your Intended Self

Notes to Self for Chapter Five

Want to work on the ideas in this chapter further? Deep Dive Exercises for Chapter Five are on Page 218.

Chapter Six

The Power of Thought: Your Subconscious Mind

Once upon a time, a Cherokee grandfather was speaking to his grandson about life.

"A fight is going on inside me," said the grandfather to his grandson. "It is a terrible fight between two wolves. One is evil. He is anger, envy, sorrow, regret, greed, arrogance, self-pity, guilt, resentment, inferiority, lies, false pride, superiority and ego. The other wolf is good. He is joy, peace, love, hope, serenity, humility, kindness, benevolence, empathy, generosity, truth, compassion and faith. This same fight is going on inside every person. The same fight is going on within you."

The grandson pondered this thought and then asked, "Which wolf will win, Grandfather?"

The grandfather replied, "The one you feed."

The next tool from the cooperative universe directing me to my intended self and my piece of the puzzle was provided by a bad back.

I suffer from a congenital back defect that led to a portion of my spine being surgically fused in my early 30s. A year after the surgery, my pain continued; I was offered more surgery. Having lost over a year of my life to the first surgery, I could not imagine having another one. I had been feeding this wolf for many years, and I wanted to stop feeding it.

Years earlier, I quit smoking with the help of a clinical psychologist who hypnotized me and taught me how to self-hypnotize. If you have ever daydreamed, you know what self-hypnosis is. We all go into a trance-like state while daydreaming; the trick with self-hypnosis or meditation is to consciously harness the trance. The process was so successful that not only did I quit, but I didn't even think of myself as a smoker – former or otherwise - anymore.

Desperate to avoid another spine surgery, I called the clinical psychologist, who taught me to self-hypnotize earlier when I quit smoking. The cooperative universe provided exactly what I needed; he was now specializing in using hypnosis and self-hypnosis for people in chronic pain.

Over the course of a year, he taught me how to turn off my pain through self-hypnosis, and he literally gave me my life back.

There were a few roadblocks during the year. While when he hypnotized me, my pain would stop. I could not stop the pain myself through self-hypnosis. Eventually, I came to see the reason I couldn't turn off the pain myself. I came to see that I thought if I could simply turn off the pain, perhaps the pain wasn't real. Perhaps this pain was something I made up. My doctor helped me see there are two kinds of pain – productive pain and unproductive pain. Productive pain calls on your body to do something. So, when you put your finger in a flame the pain you feel tells your brain to pull your finger out of the flame. The damage had already been done to my back, so I could ignore the pain message. This was unproductive pain. I got this but still couldn't hypnotize myself. Gently, he helped me see the reason I couldn't do it: I believed only he could do it. Because I had told it so, my subconscious mind believed I couldn't do it. I had created my own reality. Once he helped me create a new and different reality to suit my need to end the pain, I was able to turn off the pain using self-hypnosis and have been doing so successfully for over 25 years. My subconscious is programmable.

> Make the most of what you have. Don't feel sorry for yourself. Don't tell people when you are having a bad day or feeling badly. Act as if you are having a good day and the bad day will pass.
>
> D.H. 1922 ♀

> The most important thing in life is attitude, attitude, attitude. Know that while nothing in life is perfect and you can't have everything you want, if you roll with the punches and don't expect each day to be perfect, life will be grand.
>
> D.H. 1922♀︎

While I was hypnotized, my psychologist also led me though several visualizations where he asked me to see where my spine had been fused and visualize it becoming more solid and stable. I could visualize my spine and the area that needed more stabilization, but I couldn't make it more solid. I worked for weeks on this visualization and suddenly one day, I knew what the feeling of further fusion felt like. And, I did it. Over and over. My pain continued to lessen. Years later when reviewing an MRI of my spine, my surgeon noted he had never seen additional fusion like mine occur so long after the original surgery. Photographic proof of the power of the mind.

I was no longer defined by my problematic spine. Using the power of my subconscious mind, I was able to stop feeding that wolf.

All of us have heard the data phrase, "Garbage in; garbage out." Getting good data and results out of a computer is dependent on what you have put into it. People's brains are no different. What you put in a brain influences what comes out. Your ability to influence your thinking depends on the belief that you can do it. As Henry Ford is attributed as saying, "If you think you can or think you can't, you are right."

If you believe that your brain is programmable, you get to decide what to put in the program. You can create your own reality.

Imagine what this might look like.

> Get quiet in a comfortable chair and close your eyes. Actively relax your legs, your arms, your neck and the muscles in your face.
>
> Now picture yourself talking to a younger version of yourself. See exactly where you both are, where you are sitting and what you are wearing.
>
> Give an important piece of advice to your younger self. Say it carefully, simply and with care. Now imagine your younger self smiling and nodding their head. They like the advice and will begin using it right away.

What you have just done is a shortened form of a creative visualization, which is very like self-hypnosis, and is the first tool in your power-of-the-mind toolkit.

Our minds are made up of a conscious and a subconscious mind. The subconscious mind is like a computer; it cannot think on its own and takes at face value whatever is presented to it. It doesn't judge or evaluate. It just takes what it is given. We can program our subconscious mind by consistently presenting it with the same thought again and again. The subconscious brain accepts what

---

> Sometimes you will think you can't and you won't. Try thinking you can more often.
>
> **E.H. 1950♀**

we give it without judgment, and it will accept what we give it as reality. It then makes this vision of reality real in our lives. It selects and brings about circumstances which support the reality it knows. In this way, the thoughts we put repetitively in our subconscious mind are manifested. As a Voice of Wisdom put it:

> Choose carefully. We all get good at what we practice. Small missteps can lead to big things.
>
> D.P. 1951 ♂

When we repeatedly program our own computer, everything becomes possible.

I return to the self-hypnosis story because I was so enthused about the benefits of self-hypnosis I asked my therapist if it was advisable to teach it to my young children. He said he had already taught his kids and offered me the following story:

He had taught his ten-year old daughter to self-hypnotize slowly by first teaching her to visualize a special place of her very own. Before each bedtime, they practiced. With her eyes closed, he helped her see her special place including all sights, sounds and smells. After a week or so, she could visualize the place at will. At first she just used it for relaxation, but soon they began to explore visualizing things she might want to have happen and support with visualization. She visualized doing well on a test, having a good day at school, getting along with a difficult teacher.

One day, he got one of those dreaded calls from the school nurse. "Your daughter is alright but has a nasty gash on her forehead from falling off the swings. When she came to me there was a lot of blood. You need to come get her and take her to the emergency room as soon as possible."

The worried psychologist said he was on his way, but before the nurse signed off, she said, "One other thing I wanted to mention: she is sitting just staring out the window and won't answer my questions."

The dad smiled and asked, "Is her cut still bleeding?"

"No," the nurse answered, "I've never seen anything like it. It seems to be slowing down."

"Leave her alone," the dad replied," I'll be there in ten minutes."

The dad knew she had self-hypnotized and visualized the bleeding slowing down. And it did.

I shared this story with my children and helped them learn to self-hypnotize. We called it "going to your place", and they both got good at it.

My son became a true believer at a youth soccer game. Called on to make a penalty kick, he leaned over briefly, closed his eyes, and I knew he was visualizing the ball going right into the net. And it did! Unfortunately, one kid on his team was off-sides, and the kick had to be redone. Everything was so rushed he had no time to visualize, and he missed. The lesson had been learned though. I frequently saw him pause momentarily to visualize during much of his successful high school athletic career.

Our minds are so powerful. We need to be *mindful* of what we consciously put in them. We need to put in good things that we desire. By using the tools provided by the cooperative universe, we can control how we view the world, what we think about ourselves and others and how we react to circumstances and situations. By carefully choosing our responses to all persons, places and things, we powerfully affect our circumstance. We support the vision we desire. And that vision is becoming the person we were always intended to be.

S.M.H 1949 ♀ ䷿

Notes to Self for Chapter Six

Want to work on the ideas in this chapter further? Deep Dive Exercises for Chapter Six are on Page 220.

Chapter Seven

The Power of Thought: Affirmations

Once upon a time there was a farmer who couldn't find his old mule. While searching high and low, the farmer heard talking coming from the direction of the well. When the farmer peered into the well, he saw his mule and heard him say, "I'm going to die down here. I'm going to die down here. Woe is me; I'm going to die down here."

The farmer assessed the situation, and while he sympathized with the mule, he decided that neither the mule nor the well was worth the trouble of saving. So he called his neighbors together and enlisted them to help *haul dirt to bury the old mule in the well and put him out of his misery.*

As the dirt began to come down around him, the mule continued to say, "I'm going to die down here. I'm going to die down here. Woe is me; I'm going to die down here."

But as the farmer and his neighbors continued shoveling, a thought struck the mule. It suddenly dawned on him that every time a shovel load of dirt landed on his back, he could shake it off and step up.

"Shake it off and step up…shake it off and step up…shake it off and step up," he repeated to himself over and over, until at last tired and dirty, he reached the top of the well and was able to step out.

When I was a working mother with small children, I had no time. I said that I had no time to myself and who ever else would listen, and I said it frequently. I didn't realize it at the time, but I was using the power of my mind to reinforce that I had no time.

At a party, I mentioned to another guest that there weren't enough hours in the day for me, and she suggested, I come up with an affirmation to help me find

> Always remember the compliments you received. Forget about the rude remarks!
>
> D.R.1950♀

more time. Never having heard of them but desperate to try anything, I agreed, and she helped me come up with the phrase, "I have more than enough time to do all things I need to do." She tutored me in the power of affirmations. I started saying it like a mantra. I said it out loud when I was driving. I said it in my mind when I was dozing off to sleep. I said it under my breath when I was rushed. I put a post-it note with the affirmation on my bathroom mirror, on my kitchen window and on my dashboard.

I began to have more time.

I continued to say the affirmation.

I became a believer.

Affirmations were the next tool the cooperative universe provided on my journey to my piece of the puzzle. They are the next tool for you to harness the power of your thoughts. Back then, I would have said that I stumbled onto affirmations by accident but that was before I realized there are no accidents – just opportunities presented to me.

We all are continually talking to ourselves both consciously and unconsciously. Using affirmations allows us

> The most important thing in life is attitude, attitude, attitude. Know that while nothing in life is perfect and you can't have everything you want, if you roll with the punches and don't expect each day to be perfect, life will be grand.
>
> D.H. 1922 ♀

to consciously choose what we are saying to ourselves, and to consciously use positive self-talk. By choosing to improve your self-talk, you decide to put something other than garbage into your subconscious. You program your subconscious mind, so your thinking, conscious mind chooses to see the world as you want. All things become possible.

In general, an affirmation is a statement asserting the existence or the truth of something. If you believe that you can program your own computer, then an affirmation becomes a way to reinforce or improve something in your thinking and a way to create and then reinforce new ways of thinking. Affirmations are powerful and must be carefully chosen, formatted carefully and only then frequently repeated to oneself. For an affirmation to be effective it needs to be in the present tense, it must have a positive message, and it must be personalized and specific to your needs.

To reinforce the power of affirmations and stress how carefully they must be crafted and chosen, it should be noted that it was only later after a bout with depression, that I added "want" to my affirmation with magical results. More time for me, too.

> Stand up for yourself. Speak up!
>
> O.N. 1928 ♂

> *I have more than enough time to do all the things I want and need to do.*

While I use many affirmations, one of the most helpful has been:

> *I am a capable, competent person who can handle everything that comes my way well.*

Say that to yourself many times a day for two weeks, and you will begin to be a capable, competent person who can handle everything that comes your way - well.

Two important things to remember about affirmations. First, thinking that the problem is *out there* is a problem because you can't get someone else to say your affirmation. Only you can choose to say an affirmation. Second, believing that something isn't a problem *unless* it has a solution means you believe you can find the solution. You don't have to know what the solution is; you just need to believe there is a solution somewhere. If you believe these two things, you can take control of your own thoughts through the use of affirmations.

> Love yourself for if you don't you can't love anyone else.
>
> D.H. 1922♀

If you believe that you can program your own computer then you can create and visualize your own reality. Our conscious minds are blessed with a frontal lobe that responds to reason, so we can change the way we think by using our conscious mind to program our subconscious minds. As we create our own reality, we need to be very mindful of our choices.

Affirmations are one way to literally change our thoughts, and positive self-talk is another way to create and support healthy self-esteem. For example, if you reach the car only to realize that you forgot you wallet in the house, do you say, "Stupid me, I always forget things," or "Thank goodness I remembered my wallet before I left the driveway"? Do you tell yourself you are stupid or resourceful? Positive self-talk is a powerful positive force in the way we view ourselves and the world. Begin to notice the words you say and the thoughts you think. Are they the ones you choose now? If not, begin to devise your personal talking points and affirmations.

Here is a short list of time tested affirmations. More are listed in the Appendix. Some people suggest you say them at least a hundred times daily, or that you should say them convincingly in front of a mirror. I found affirmations written on sticky notes to be great reminders. Find what work for you.

- *Every day in every way, I'm getting better and better.*
- *It is easy for me to be grateful for who I am and the life I live.*
- *I am grateful to life for all that I have received until now and for all that I will be receiving in the future.*

- *All is well. Everything that is happening is for my highest good.*

Your next step to find your puzzle piece is to choose an affirmation and begin saying it. Say it until it is as automatic as breathing. Which will you choose? Will you write your own? I know you will handle this assignment well because remember, you are *a capable, competent person who can handle everything that comes your way well.*

Notes to Self for Chapter Seven

Want to work on the ideas in this chapter further? Deep Dive Exercises for Chapter Seven are on Page 222.

Chapter Eight

The Power of Thought: Personal Talking Points

In one of my jobs, I was responsible for communications and public relations (PR). One of the duties of a PR person is writing talking points for spokespeople. If you have ever seen a politician or CEO interviewed on TV, and said to yourself, "They didn't really answer that question," blame it on talking points. The PR person decides what messages they want to get across in the interview, writes them out in simple form, gives them to the spokesperson, and tells him/her, "No matter what the question, answer with one of these talking points." It is called "managing the message". I would suggest you become your own personal PR person, so you can learn to manage your own messages.

The next powerful tool is to establish and use personal talking points. Throughout this book, you may notice several recurring themes. I think of these themes as things I know for sure. These things I know for sure are my personal talking points.

> If you believe what you are saying, you will be believed.
>
> M.H. 1955 ♂

As my own personal PR person, I created my personal talking points. Things that I know for sure. Things that can be used when just about any question comes up. Things that can reinforce positive self-talk and support affirmations. Crafting personal talking points was the next tool provided by the cooperative universe to support me as I became my intended self and discovered my piece in the puzzle. In this book, I share my talking points with you, and I share how they became my talking points. You may agree or disagree with them. I hope you know by now your agreement with my ideas isn't what matters. What matters is your finding your own. Take mine as an example, begin to believe personal talking points support your journey to your intended self and start thinking about what your talking points are as you examine mine.

Here are the first five of my fourteen personal talking points:

> Treasure the people in your life...
> they won't always be there.
>
> O.H. 1920 ♂

Personal Talking Point Number One: The only things I truly own and control are contained in my brain. I will therefore learn as much as I can and guard against putting garbage in.

Personal Talking Point Number Two: We are all on a journey, and we all have lessons to learn on this journey. If we open ourselves up, the cooperative universe always provides exactly what we need to learn, grow and discover the reason we are here.

Personal Talking Point Number Three: The universe constantly provides opportunities for growth; therefore, I am open to them. Difficult circumstances often create paradigm shifts, whole new frames of reference by which people see themselves, the world, others in the world and what life is asking of them. I will therefore not fear difficult circumstances because of the opportunities they bring.

Personal Talking Point Number Four: People create and visualize their own reality. Knowing I am responsible for all my reactions to all persons, places and things, I choose my responses carefully, thus powerfully affecting my circumstance and helping to create my own reality. I know that thinking the problem is "out there" is a problem.

Personal Talking Point Number Five: People believe what you tell them. One good story is worth more than any amount of research.

Personal talking points can be used to reinforce a belief system — a belief system that is of your own choosing. They can be used to support thought patterns you want. Here is how I used the first five personal talking points to reprogram my computer:

Personal Talking Point Number One: The only things I truly own and control are contained in my brain. I will therefore learn as much as I can and guard against putting garbage in.

Ask anyone who has experienced loss due to a fire, tornado or hurricane, and they will tell you that anything you physically own can be lost. I have lost many things in my life I once thought vital to my well being. They were not. Knowing that the only thing I cannot lose is within the space between my ears makes me seek out and choose positive things to put in there.

Personal Talking Point Number Two: We are all on a journey, and we all have lessons to learn on this journey. If we open ourselves up, the cooperative universe always provides exactly what we need to learn, grow and discover the reason we are here.

The belief that if we open ourselves up that the cooperative universe always provides exactly what we need to learn and grow gives me the confidence that there are reasons for the problems I encounter on my journey, and there are solutions to those problems. It also gives me confidence that I will get support from the cooperative universe to find those solutions. This means that instead of tossing and turning all night over some problem, I can repeat this talking point to myself and slow the spinning of my brain, confident that the answers will come.

> Relationships will fade if you don't nourish them, and you won't believe how rewarding they are as you get older. So make the effort and stay in touch. Family, friends, and buncups are beyond price.
>
> T.R. 1949 ♂

Personal Talking Point Number Three: The universe constantly provides opportunities for growth; therefore, I am open to them. Difficult circumstances often create paradigm shifts, whole new frames of reference by which people see themselves, the world, others in the world and what life is asking of them. I will therefore not fear difficult circumstances because of the opportunity they bring.

Instead of fearing difficulties, with the support and clarity of this personal talking point I can learn to welcome them. It is through mistakes that we learn, and you need to be a learning machine on this journey. If I need to have a difficult conversation with a person I fear, I can repeat this personal talking point to myself before the conversation and calm myself knowing that no matter what the outcome of the conversation, there is a lesson for me. It also helps me address difficulties more quickly because of the promise they bring.

One lesson came from my parents, who grew up during the Depression and were greatly influenced by it. They liked a clean plate, they hated to buy on credit and they always needed a little cash in their pocket to feel secure. Out of love for me, they sheltered me from the harsh realities of money. In hindsight, it is clear they went too far. At one point when I was 12 years old, they asked where I wanted to go to dinner. I responded, "Let's go to the country club, it is free there." They programmed my computer to believe that I didn't need to worry my pretty little head about money. Money management has been a lesson the universe has presented to me many times, and I am proud to say, I have made many improvements in my relationship with money.

There have been many personal opportunities for growth from the cooperative universe. An unanticipated, not-fun divorce helped me learning to stand on my own two feet. Executing both my parents' living wills under trying circumstances led to a closer relationship with both of them. The collapse of a family company put me on a path to an interesting and successful career. My life only makes sense looking backward, for I could never have planned the twists and turns it took. Twists and turns provided the lessons and have informed my Talking Points. Begin to see the difficulties in your life as neither good nor bad but merely something you can use to propel you in the direction you want to head.

Personal Talking Point Number Four: People create and visualize their own reality. Knowing I am responsible for all my reactions to all persons, places and things, I choose my responses carefully, thus powerfully affecting my circumstance and helping to create my own reality. I know thinking the problem is "out there" is a problem.

> Be sure that there are at least two people in this world that you would die for and at least 15 people in this world that you love in some way.
>
> A.A. 1930♀

As I think carefully about what my responses are to all persons, places and things are, I powerfully affect my circumstance. Part of this is being responsible for our actions, but it goes beyond that. If I am responsible for my responses to all people, places and things, the impact is broader. For example, this means I can choose to be kind to a person I dislike. I can't change my feelings, and this is in no way a suggestion to stuff or ignore your feelings, but you can be responsible for your actions towards that person.

Let's say my boss has just given me an unwarranted bad review that stems from his personal political agenda at work. I still need to work with him closely on a project important to us both. Knowing that my reaction will set the tone for the meeting and that I can control my reaction to him, I choose to be polite and professional during our meetings, even though I am feeling far from polite and professional. I continue to repeat this personal talking point until I can clearly see the logical solution to this problem.

Personal Talking Point Number Five: People believe what you tell them. One good story is worth more than any amount of research.

If you can program your computer (subconscious mind), you can also program other people's computers. Imagine that I have just lost my job. Panic sets in. If I believe that the universe constantly provides opportunities for growth, I could say to myself, I am open to this because I know difficult circumstances often create paradigm shifts, whole new frames of reference by which people see the world and themselves and others in it and what life is asking of them. I will therefore not fear difficult circumstances because of the opportunity they bring. Some people believe that before a shift, the cooperative universe gives you a wilderness zone, a time of not-knowing, before the paradigm shift occurs. The wilderness zone is an uncomfortable place. If I lost my job, I would say Personal Talking Point Number Five to myself. I would say it in some form to anyone who asked if I was worried. I would try to get used to the discomfort of the wilderness. Harkening back to Personal Talking Point Number Four, I know I can create *and visualize* my own *reality;* I will *choose my responses to all persons, places and things,* and warm up the resume and start networking. Networking means interaction with others, so the next step is Personal Talking Point Number Five.

Knowing that people believe what you tell them, when asked about my job loss, I say, "I liked the job I had but now see it was really time for a change and am really looking forward to my next opportunity. If I had my druthers I would have chosen the time to leave myself, but I now see this was the kick in the butt I needed to make a change, so I am grateful."   What kind of reaction will you get from managing your message this way? No doubt a positive one. I am no Pollyanna here, but I do know people believe what you tell them, so be mindful what you say. If you manage your message, you are more likely to get the response you desire and the support you need.

> Be truthful and keep your friends as long as you can.
>
> W.S. 1936 ♂

A few words about feelings. Researchers at University of California Long Beach confirmed what Nat King Cole made popular in a song. [ii]   If you "smile even when you heart is breaking," you'll soon find that life is all worthwhile. In other words, faking it can help you make it. So, while feelings need to be understood and felt, what we can and need to control is what we *do* with the feelings.

Imagine a kindergarten room. One kid reaches over and takes a toy from another kid. For the kid minus the toy, shock and anger are probably appropriate feelings at this point. But a good teacher gives the child some options as to what to do with those feelings, perhaps including asking for its return or getting another toy. She also points out that biting the offending kid isn't a viable option.

We too get to choose what we do with our feelings.

Let's say you just lost your job and are feeling discouraged. You say to people, "Man, I just lost my job, and it was a great job that I really liked. I don't think I will ever be able to find a job like that one again. I may not be able to find any job again."

Knowing people generally believe what you tell them, what will their reaction be? Most likely something like, "Wow, that is awful. In this economy, I have heard of people being out of work for years. You must really be bummed."

And, because your subconscious mind just takes things in and doesn't judge, you believe what people tell you; you feel bummed. This cycle of feeling bad was started by the person who lost the job and was reinforced by the listener. This is a downward spiral.

Knowing you can control your message and that people tend to believe what you tell them, instead you say, "Yeah, I lost my job, but I am really excited about finding something that will utilize all the skills I gained during my time with the company. I learned a lot about marketing in my role in communications, and I am anxious to find a job that allows me to use that skill set. People are always looking for marketing help." The response may be, "That is great! I know some people in marketing. I could ask if they'd talk to you about the field."

This cycle of feeling hopeful and positive was started by the person who lost the job and reinforced by the listener, which makes the person who lost the job feel more hopeful.

Parents have an especially strong influence on how a child views him or herself because they tell the child who he or she is from an early age thus programming their brain. If you were lucky and raised by June and Ward Cleaver, you may have gotten good positive views of yourself. But perhaps you learned some bad messages about yourself from your parents. Remember: there is no license required to become a parent, so if you fall into this category, you aren't alone.

Phrases like, "You aren't smart enough to do that," "That is a stupid idea," "Are you crazy?" "Only boys do that," "You are really weird," program our brains so we believe we are stupid, crazy and weird. Consciously or not, your parents told you who you were and may have held up a distorted mirror into which you looked. Remember, your conscious mind doesn't evaluate, it just absorbs information. You can reprogram, or re-parent, your conscious brain with positive messages.

If you hate your apartment because it is small and doesn't face the good light in the east, you can choose to find something you like about it each day, thus strongly impacting your reaction. Harnessing our powerful frontal lobes help us change our view.

Imagine your apartment is not perfect.

Imagine you are having coffee with your friend, and the topic of your apartment comes up. If you said, "I hate my apartment. It is too small and has bad light," your friend would not only agree with you – because people believe what you tell them – but she would also most likely fan the flame of discontent and respond, " I don't know how you live in this lightless, small place."

The downward spiral is reinforced.

Or, knowing that *People believe what you tell them. One good story is worth more than any amount of research,* you decide to choose differently. Imagine the same friend, the same coffee, the same conversation, only this time you say," I like my apartment. It is cozy. But, I am thinking about looking for something new. I had one friend who wrote down everything she wanted in an apartment then spent one day going to open houses for apartments that had those features, and she found the perfect match in one day." She would most likely say, "That so sounds like something you would do! I like your apartment too. Once you find something new, I wouldn't mind talking it off your hands."

OK, it doesn't always work just that way, but you see my point. Manage your message to support an upward, positive spiral.

I was having a conversation with a colleague, who mentioned he was getting a divorce; his second. He said he worried about what people would think, specifically that they could think him foolish, stupid and/or hard to get along with. After a long discussion I asked him if he was happier now that it was over. He quickly said that he had never felt better, and it was a good decision to get the divorce. I mentioned that while I was glad to hear his concerns about people's reactions, if he was truly concerned about their reactions, he should share only the last part: "Never felt better, and it was a good decision to get the divorce." I told him that *people believe what you tell them*. He tried it and people responded as most people would, saying, "Good for you!" He felt uncomfortable with the situation but also was being responsible for his reactions and managing his message, so he got what he needed: encouragement and an upward spiral.

Our thoughts can be made more powerful through creative visualization, affirmations and personal talking points – all of which help us use positive self-talk and manage our message. The universe wants each of us to have happy, healthy lives, to enjoy our own and the company of others and to find our puzzle piece. We can harness the power of thought to work with the cooperative universe to accomplish these things.

Notes to Self for Chapter Eight

Want to work on the ideas in this chapter further? Deep Dive Exercises for Chapter Eight are on Page 224.

Chapter Nine
The Power of People: Together We Are an Ocean

*I*n junior high, I was given an assignment to interview my parents about World War II and write about what I learned. While I needed to be older before I understood exactly how extraordinary my parent's contributions were, it was during this assignment that I learned about their commitment to "the war effort."

My parents were in their mid to late twenties at the beginning of the war, and both stopped the paths of their lives – in my mother's case, a career in human resources, and in my father's case, the timeline of his work to become a physician – to support the war effort.

As many others of their generation, they sacrificed for the greater good.

The junior reporter in me asked, "Why?" In answer, both independently used the same phrase: "Individually, we are one drop. Together, we are an ocean."

Focusing on a common goal is powerful, and the first step in mediation is to find a common goal for the warring parties. If they can agree on a common end goal – for example, the well being of the children in a contentious divorce - they can focus on that goal and agree to the smaller steps needed to get there.

The greatest generation focused on a common goal and accepted the smaller personal steps it took to get there.

> A smile from you can bring happiness to anyone, even if they don't like you.
>
> A.B. 1932 ♂

Each of us is on a journey to find our place in the puzzle; how we fit into that something larger. On this journey, we are constantly interacting with other pieces in the puzzle, each on their own journey to find their piece. Each of these interactions becomes a part of our journey. We always need to remember that we are all part of the same puzzle, and the puzzle wants all pieces in place. All the pieces in the puzzle are interconnected. At a minimum, this means each of must be respectful to the other pieces, and ideally, we must cooperate with other pieces. If we are all part of the same puzzle, then the overarching idea to keep in mind when we interact with others is that we are all one. If you believe this, it would follow that what we do to others, we do also to ourselves. It would, therefore, make sense to treat others as we would want to be treated. Our common goal is the completion of the puzzle; individually, we are one drop, together, we are an ocean.

Keep this affirmation as you think about your interactions:

> *I am completely responsible for all my reactions to all people, places and things.*

Sarvepalli Radhakrishnan, former president of India, believed that each of us should love our neighbor as ourselves because we are our neighbor; he believed that it is only an illusion that makes us think that our neighbor is someone other than ourselves.[iii] This golden rule concept appears in some form in most religions:

- Buddhism: "Hurt not others with that which pains yourself." [iv]
- Judaism: "Thou shalt love thy neighbor as thyself." [v]
- Zoroastrianism: "Whatever is disagreeable to yourself, do not do unto others." [vi]

- Confucianism:" What you do not want done to yourself, do not do to others." [vii]
- Hinduism: "One should always treat others as they themselves wish to be treated." [viii]
- Christianity: "So in everything, do to others what you would have them do to you, for this sums up the Law and the Prophets.[ix]

Think of how your mindset might change if you thought all things were actually a part of you. How would you treat another person? How would you treat another person who was driving you nuts? How would you treat another person who disagreed with you? Remember – on a cellular level that other person is you. If both good, positive energy and bad, negative energy persist and flow back to you, which one would you choose to have around you? Which would you choose to radiate back to you?

> People are not things, and everyone has a right to be treated with dignity.
>
> P.B. 1933 ♂

The puzzle is made up of many pieces. As we discover the size, shape, color, content and purpose of our piece of the puzzle, there are nearly 70 billion people doing exactly the same thing in their own fashion. While we are on our journey we are interacting with them on theirs. Some of these interactions are brief, and some endure. But short or long, all of these interactions and the people in them are a part of us and can either help us towards our goal or get in the way of our journey to find our piece of the puzzle. And we get to choose whether each interaction and each relationship will help or hurt our progress.

Knowing this, while we search for our unique role in this lifetime, our unique piece of the puzzle, we need also to look at the entire puzzle – the rest of the continually recycled stuff that is also part of us. This larger force has all the force of the entire universe and can play a beneficial or detrimental role in our journey. The question is – do you want to do this the hard way or the easy way? Do you want to work with the power of the universe or against it?

When we step back and look at the entire puzzle, we see its size and its force. If we are all one in this cooperative universe, then think of the power behind this force. If we open ourselves up to this force, the whole power of the cooperative universe gets behind us. We can either work with this power or resist it. Knowing the power of the cooperative universe, I think the smart money would be on the former. Open your self up to the power of the cooperative universe and start attracting the good stuff that comes from putting out and working with the good stuff.

> Look out for people who have less than you do.
>
> J.W. 1967 ♂

As I began developing my personal talking points, it was not surprising that some pertained to interacting with others. Talking Points Number Six through Eight are pertinent to the area of relationships:

Personal Talking Point Number Six: Everything in this world is influenced by people. I will therefore, treat all people with respect and tolerance. What goes around comes around.

Personal Talking Point Number Seven: People are capable of change, but people will only do things that are important to them. Being important to me doesn't translate into the same thing being important to them.

Personal Talking Point Number Eight: A person can create a vision of another person that impacts how they perceive themselves. Therefore, I will be a light, not a judge and a model, not a critic. I will surround myself with people who value me and make my perceptions more accurate.

> I know you aren't going to church, but I am sure you know that old Bible verse, "We are all one in Jesus Christ." Remember that when you think you are better than someone else.
>
> K.J. 1938 ♀

One of my 60th year transformations was to stop having expectations of others. Here is how these three talking points, individually and in combination, led me to reprogram my computer and make this transformation.

Personal Talking Point Number Six: Everything in this world is influenced by people. I will therefore, treat all people with respect and tolerance. What goes around comes around.

This is an acknowledgement that while each person on a cellular level is part of me. Each of them is also on a journey of their own. Each of them is being supported by the cooperative universe – *whether or not they or I can see that support.* At the point we interact with them they already may have been presented a lesson many times. They may be on the cusp of learning from the lesson. Even though we are all one, no one can know another's journey. I can support them but not lead another. I can listen and let them know what is true for me, but I can not lecture and let them know what they should do. For this reason, I will concentrate not on their journey but on the one over which I can have the most influence – *my own.* By allowing others progress on their journey, the cooperative universe allows me progress on mine.

During my 60th year, I also decided I have no expectation of how they will receive my respect and my tolerance. I know the only part I control is my commitment to giving them to each person.

I believe that part of my piece of the puzzle is to help others find theirs. Before I gave up having expectations of others, I tended to try to control others when I saw them going down what I believed to be the wrong path. I

> Two trips to the delivery room and way too many trips to funerals will help you see what is important and the importance of having your relationships in order.
>
> **H.M. 1957 ♂**

now see this meddling as my misinterpretation of what I was born to do. My meddling was a perversion of my goal to help others find their path. I had the goal right, but the vehicle wrong. I was attempting to be a "universe coordinator." I see now that not only was it an exhausting job; I also wasn't very good at it.

On some level I wanted the others in my life to not cause me pain. I didn't like the pain of seeing loved ones make mistakes or experience pain themselves, but this was something I could not control. Instead, I decided to let go of this expectation by choosing another response. When I saw a loved one going down a path that would cause them (and me) pain, I stopped interfering with their opportunity to discover the joy and self-confidence that can accompany personal achievement and the growth that can come from failure. I turned their journey over to them and the cooperative universe.

> When you are younger and running around with the crowd, don't feel like you have to do what the crowd does. A lot of times the best thing to do is to get out of the crowd. I started smoking to be part of the crowd and didn't quit until I was an old man.
>
> N.D.E 1920 ♂

Personal Talking Point Number Seven: People are capable of change, but people will only do things that are important to them. Being important to me doesn't make them important to someone else.

During couple's counseling prior to my divorce, I asked the therapist if people could change. After some thought, he replied, "I believe they can in the same way that a

S.M.H 1949 ♀ 冨

drowning man who does not know how to swim can sometimes find his way to shore." Then he added, "But he has to know he is drowning."

When I was still in my ill-fated universe coordinator role, I used to believe I knew what was right for another person, and was frequently generous enough to share that with them. I knew when they were drowning, which way shore was and how to teach them to swim. As a parent, when my children were small. I could usually get them to do what I wanted them to do. As they got older, I learned I could get them to do what I wanted them to as long as they were within my physical reach. It was then I learned children need to develop their own internal parent. So when crossing the street alone, they know to look both ways before crossing —even though the one who taught them isn't there. I now know I can not make a drowning person know he is drowning —nor should I. Mark Twain is credited with saying that if you hold a cat by the tail you learn things you cannot learn any other way. The lesson will be presented until it is learned.

During my 60th year, I decided to no longer have expectations about people changing who they are and what they do. I know the only part I control is whether I want to change who I am and what I do.

> Mr. Rodgers liked you just the way you are. Don't you think it would help if you did as he said with other people?
>
> B.G. 1950♀

89

Personal Talking Point Number Eight: A person can create a vision of another person that impacts how they perceive themselves. Therefore, I will be a light, not a judge and a model, not a critic. I will surround myself with people who value me and make my perceptions more accurate.

Most of us underestimate the power of our words on other people. To illustrate, think of the last time you spent time with a positive person - a person who finds something good in everything including you. Then compare that to the last time you spent with a negative person —a person who finds something negative in everything including you. Do you even need to think about which person you would prefer to re-visit?

Human behavior is contagious. Human behavior is viral. Negative behavior breeds negativity, and positive behavior breeds positivity. In an effort to support another person on their journey, I will take my role in others lives seriously by being a light and a positive model. Knowing that people believe what you tell them, I will look for positive things to say. To take care of myself and get needed support for my journey, I will choose the same type of person for me.

> What goes around comes around is true. Treat others as you would like to be treated. It may take awhile, but it will come back to you.
>
> L.L. 1948 ♂

During my 60th year, I decided to no longer be a judge or a critic of others. I remind myself they are also supported by the cooperative universe on their journey, and since I do not know where they are on that journey, I am in no position to judge.

I do not, however, have the expectation that others have decided the same thing. For this reason I will choose to be around people who value me. I will carefully think about the people with whom I spend time. I will not spend time with people who make me feel bad about myself. I will choose to spend time with those that make me feel better. Whether they are acquaintances, friends or family members, I know I can not change them. I know the only part I control is my reaction to people.

The rest of this chapter is divided into sections about friends, family, partnerships and relationships overall, as are the Notes to Self following each. There are deep dive exercises at the end of the book for each of four sections in this chapter that ask you to look at what our Voices of Wisdom said about each of these areas individually. Each deep dive asks you to be curious about how the people in your life can best nurture and be a support to your journey; not impede your progress.

> Don't listen to people who say you can't do it!
>
> J.W. 1967 ♂

Friends

Voices of Wisdom on Friends

Life gets better. So you're not the most popular person in high school —you're one of those people who has a few close friends. Treasure them —they'll get you through and beyond. Believe me, in 20 years, no matter what clique people belonged to, you'll be happy to see each other at your high school reunion.

M.M. 1963 ♀

Make friends and keep them. They are a lasting treasure.

D.H. 1922 ♀

Don't worry about who doesn't like you, who has more, or who's doing what. Instead, let's cherish the relationships you have with those who do love you.

E.B. 1934 ♀

Men come and go . . . female friends last a lifetime.

P.S. 1949 ♀

When life hands you Lemons, ask for tequila and salt and call a friend.

J.C. 1952 ♂

You can never have too many friends. Try to accumulate them throughout your life and then hold onto them as long as you can. When pressed for time and you must make a choice, choose the path that lets you work, play, find, cultivate and live with friends. It will make the days seem shorter and the experience richer.

T.E. 1953 ♂

It really is who you know not what you know, so stay in touch with your friends!

M.K. 1925 ♂

If I had known while I was a teenager that friends were the most important part of life, I would have been more open to making friends. That habit of slow communication has remained throughout my life. Now it is hard to overcome a lifetime habit. But if I realize what a big effect it has on my everyday life, you will need to develop more good ways of communication with the people you meet regularly. What exactly these habits are is what you need to concentrate on —respond immediately to greetings, with comment or question about their well-being, then comments about what's happening, questions about what's happening with them. Questions like did you see that movie? Comments about what they read recently that is important to them and perhaps you, too. What did you do with your holiday? Follow up with pertinent comments in response to what they say. In other words, be more interested, honestly, about their life. In the beginning, it will seem like prying but you need to overcome that reluctance. They will indicate, somehow, that they aren't willing to respond and don't want to. You need to become skillful in reading facial expressions for what they really mean. Also, you must be willing to spend timeout of your busy life for events that bring "us" into intimate and friendly situations. More than anything else, you need a sincere commitment to these ideas. Good luck for both our sakes!

B.A.J 1931♀

To me at age 21: Even though you are really good at entertaining yourself and being alone, keep in touch with other people. Reach out to other people more—have a social life!

K.A. 1962♀

Invite friends over to dinner even if the carpet was stained.

E.B. 1934♀

Our Voices of Wisdom support the importance of friends and the importance of keeping them close. And, knowing that friends have a journey of their own and knowing that I *can create a vision of another person that impacts how they perceive themselves, I will be a light, not a judge and a model, not a critic.* Do I think my friend is in a dead end job? I will model the importance of a good job by having a good job myself. I will respond to her only when specifically asked, and will not be critical, preachy or didactic. I remember I have learned more from my bad bosses than I have from my good ones. I will allow her to have her own journey.

> I would not put my wishes on my daughter. She needed to have her own dreams.
>
> H.E. 1920♀

Is it hard? Yes. Does it work to get them to do what I want them to do? Only in as much as I can continue to be a part of their journey.

When I am really having trouble giving up my role as judge and critic, I find a way to be positive I imagine all the light and power of the universe surrounding my friend like a blanket. The light of the universe is no doubt a more powerful influence than I will ever be.

Unlike our families, we can choose friends. If a person is known by the company he/she keeps, you need only look to who your friends are to know who you are. Knowing this, *I will surround myself with people who value me and make my perceptions more accurate.*

When I was a single mother in graduate school, I was always short of time especially for myself. Extrovert that I was, I reached out to friends but found I felt no better. When I shared this with an older woman who had a career and a family her whole life, she asked me what my friends did for a living. Most were stay-at-home moms, who naturally had not walked in my shoes and had little understanding of my situation. I began to consciously seek out friends who were doing something similar to me and were more understanding of my circumstance; I found them not only sympathetic, but also very helpful at sharing coping skills.

I am not suggesting your friends need to be clones of you. I am suggesting if you have friends who don't understand your circumstances or don't understand your dreams, they may get in the way of progress on your journey.

Think of two people to whom you would recommend this book. Think of two that you wouldn't. Which of them will be able to hold up a more accurate mirror for you? Act accordingly.

My advice to my younger self about friends would be:

> Choose your friends wisely. Ask yourself if you feel better after time with them. If not, perhaps they aren't really friends. Choose them wisely and then help them understand how they can support you.
>
> S.M.H 1949 ♀

Notes to Self for Friends

Want to work on the ideas in this chapter further? Deep Dive Exercises for Chapter Nine: Friends are on Page 226.

Family

Voices of Wisdom on Family

Pay attention to what your elders say. They might just know something you don't

A.O. 1920 ♂

Pay more attention to your parents. They have much to teach you when you are young and when you are old.

C.A. 1922 ♂

Never say to your kids when they hugged you out of the blue, "Later. Now go get washed up for dinner."

E.B. 1934 ♀

It is perfectly OK to not be like your siblings. You compete only with yourself.

R.M. 1922 ♂

Listen more carefully to what people are saying. My adult children told me I wasn't a good listener with them.

M.A. 1920 ♀

If you can't have children, seriously consider adopting. You might be lonely without them.

D.H. 1922 ♀

Appreciate your parents. Thank them for their sacrifices on your behalf. Even if you are sure they already know you appreciate them. If you don't, you'll wish you had. Guaranteed.

T.R. 1949 ♂

Work at having good relationships with your kids, so when they need your advice, they will ask you for it.

H.A. 1923 ♀

Forgive your mom.

L.H. 1942 ♀

Don't believe it when your father says you are stupid and won't amount to anything

M.M. 1925 ♀

Look ahead . . . your sometimes difficult kids give you wonderful grandchildren.

F.M. 1931 ♂

Listen to your grandfather ramble about his youth.

E.B. 1934 ♀

No one knows where your hot buttons are better than your family, and I know I am not the only one who reverts to a younger self when interacting with my family of origin. But our Voices of Wisdom tell us our families have something for us and we should be grateful for your family, whether or not they support us in our journeys.

It helps me to think that each of my family members was chosen for a specific reason on my journey, and remember that difficult situations are opportunities for me move along on my journey from this chart to the next on my journey. Say it again. *I am completely responsible for all my reactions to all people, places and things.*

> Realize that the way your mom "loves" isn't really love. Her lack of ability to love is about her not about you. Give up trying to please her or win her love. You are lovable just as you are and a much nicer person that she is.
>
> B.J. 1950♀

As our adviser said so eloquently above, some families are so toxic they need to be avoided. But remember, they are also a part of you, so distance yourself if you must but try to distance yourself with love and respect. If you have had or are having difficulties with family, I highly recommend therapy. Parents and siblings had a great deal of power programming our computers while we were young, and sometimes we are just too close to the situation to have the perspective a qualified therapist can supply.

Whether or not you have a supportive family, you always can create the family you always wanted. Some call

S.M.H 1949 ♀ 扇

them family of the heart not the genes. I have several sisters by choice, one brother by choice, and an uncle and aunt by choice, each of whom cares for me and supports me — without the baggage.

Peace in the Puzzle: Becoming Your Intended Self

Notes to Self for Family

Want to work on the ideas in this chapter further? Deep Dive Exercises for Chapter Nine: Family are on Page 227.

Marriage and Partnerships
Voices of Wisdom on Marriage and Partnerships

Dance whenever you can. If you marry a man because he is a good dancer, you might have a good marriage or your marriage might fail, but at least you'll have had fun dancing.

D.H. 1922 ♀

Stay with your wife and family. You'll lose a lot to just go out with the guys.

N.D.E 1926 ♂

Keep your wedding vows, or don't get married. In fact, keep all your promises, or don't make them. Your regret for being a faithless shit will grow rather than fade as you get older.

T.R. 1949 ♂

When you get married you need to think like a man. Need to put away your life as a kid.

E.A. 1930 ♂

Look closely at who you marry.

B.P. 1939 ♂

Get your fun out of life before you settle down.

D.E. 1929 ♂

Maybe don't get married so young.

D.N. 1930 ♀

I did not discover my power as a woman until I was 45 years old and divorcing. I dated only rarely when I was young and never felt confident or comfortable in the dating arena. I never fully understood why and it was a great source of pain in those days. I only had a couple of relationships and would probably never have married my first husband if I had dated more or had more relationships. So, I would tell my younger self, there will be a good side to this —you will have an extra decade of independence before you marry and more opportunity to develop individually than you would have in an early marriage.

C.O. 1949 ♀

It's just as easy to fall in love with a wealthy woman as a poor one.

K.O. 1949 ♂

> Beware the love that's comfortable right from the start, because the timing is right, because your parents like him, because he makes you laugh, because it all just "works" so easily that happiness is effortless. Because real love, the knock-your-socks off, soul-mate kind of love, throws you off your stride, forces you to take a detour from your life plan. It is inconvenient, impossible to explain to your family and its accommodation demands a major life overhaul. If you find "real" love when you are young, consider yourself blessed. And if you find "real" love later in life, after you have established a family and career with their many expectations and obligations… your grief will be great, but consider yourself blessed as well.
>
> K.J. 1957 ♀

> Be sure you can support yourself before you get married… then you have your own independence to fall back on.
>
> J.L. 1932 ♀

> If possible, stay friends with your former spouses. It's unbelievably satisfying. And flattering, especially when you don't deserve it.
>
> T.R. 1949 ♂

For most of history, marriage was an economic convenience with most of the benefit going to the man. It has frequently been seen as an inherently difficult situation. In Corinthians 7:7, an unmarried Apostle Paul — believing that the second coming was imminent— counseled early Christians to stay unmarried. And, while the Buddha never spoke against marriage, he pointed out the problems, difficulties and worries people face in marriage. For him, becoming married implied a person was more attached to the physical world than the spiritual world, so it would be natural that problems would arise. [x] In *The Power of Myth*,[xi] Joseph Campbell writes that the notion of romance didn't exist until medieval times, when the troubadours began to sing of courtly love. So, if your expectation of marriage is the romanticized version, you need to know this is a fairly recent development.

> Don't be in such a hurry to get married.
> **M.M. 1930 ♀**

Anyone who has been married knows every marriage involves compromise. Reverend Joel Gibson, former dean of St. Mark's Episcopal Cathedral, wisely points this out during premarital counseling. For a marriage to be successful, each person in it needs to have a passion. For it is inevitable each will have to make compromises around his/her passion during the marriage, and it is only in this way the other understands the importance of the sacrifice being made.

> Falling in love is easy — staying in love takes work.
> **C.A. 1971 ♂**

While compromises are inherent, it is important both people be interested and invested in the growth of the other. Each person needs to be committed to the other's discovery of the authentic, essential self, or at least get out of the other person's way.

No two marriages are alike and everyone needs and wants something different from a partnership. If you are in a committed relationship, ask yourself the question – does my mate wish the best for me on my journey?

Notes to Self for Marriage and Partnerships

Want to work on the ideas in this chapter further? Deep Dive Exercises for Chapter Nine: Marriage and Partnerships are on Page 228.

Overall Relationships

How can we find and keep the good relationships we need?

We learned about the power of thought in an earlier chapter. Positive thoughts can reprogram our computer, but they also engage the cooperative universe. The cooperative universe will mirror the reality we radiate. If we radiate positivity, the universe will radiate positivity back. If you want a good relationship, try the affirmations that follow to attract the positive force of the cooperative universe. In so doing, you will become a more loving person and attract more and more loving people in your life. The cycle of positivity begins.

Affirmations:

- *All my relationships are long lasting and loving.*
- *In life, I always get what I give out and I always give out love.*
- *I deserve love and I get it in abundance.*
- *People are good. The best is yet to come.*

One of the transformations of my 60th year was to stop having expectations of others. I needed to do this with friends, with family and with all my relationships. How did I know this? I looked at my tracks in the snow. How many times was I hurt by another person's decisions? How many times did I repeat myself to someone who didn't want my advice? How many times did I try to manipulate people into my way of thinking?

Many.

I think one of my unconscious talking points used to be — I am completely responsible for the happiness of others. Ugh. I shudder just thinking about it now and hate to give it life by writing it down.

How did I stop this behavior?

I realized at the core I was behaving this way because of the way I thought. I thought people should be smart enough to realize that my ideas for them were helpful. I expected them to realize I was right. I wanted to spare them the pain of heading the wrong way and doing the wrong thing. I thought I knew what they needed to learn and how they needed to learn it. I believed I had great impact over others, despite lots of evidence to the contrary.

Perhaps if I had been more successful in my role as universe coordinator, I wouldn't have given it up. But I wasn't successful. So I changed my thinking.

S.M.H 1949 ♀ ䷑

When I truly realized the "mistakes" I had made were important parts of my journey, I became committed to allowing others to make mistakes of their own. When I realized that no amount of wishing was going to change someone else's behavior, I trusted the cooperative universe to step in. When I learned to expect nothing and hope for everything, I delighted in another's success and could commiserate with their failures without blame. When I realized that expectations are resentments in the making, I stopped having expectations.

I was better at this with friends than with family. I am confident I am better with both and better at catching myself than I used to be. Besides *acting as if,* I utilized the following affirmations:

> When you make the biggest mistake ever, something good comes from it.
>
> O.A. 1923 ♂

- *I follow the principle of "live and let live".*
- *I have compassion and kindness for all.*
- *It is easy for me to allow others to move successfully though their journeys just as I move though mine.*
- *I trust my loved one has the same support of the cooperative universe that I do.*

I am completely responsible for all my reactions to all people —this includes friends, family members and partners—*places and things.* Choose the reactions that support your journey and allow others to have their own.

Notes to Self for Overall Relationships

Want to work on the ideas in this chapter further? Deep Dive Exercises for Chapter Nine: Overall Relationships are on Page 229.

S.M.H 1949 ♀ 畺

Chapter Ten

Harness the Power of People: Your Personal Board of Directors

O nce upon a time, an old man lived alone on his small vegetable farm. He needed to spade his potato garden, but since he was a very old man and it was very hard work, he knew he couldn't manage it alone.

Unfortunately, his only son was the only person who would have helped him, and he was in prison. The old man sent his son an email that said, "I am feeling pretty bad because without your help I won't be able to plant my potato garden this year. I'm just getting too old to be digging up a garden plot. If you were here, all my troubles would be over. If only you weren't in prison."

Within minutes, the old man received an email from his son that said, 'For Heaven's sake, Dad, don't dig up the garden!! That's where I buried the money!'

Before the sun came up on the following morning, a dozen police officers showed up at the farm. After providing the confused old man a search warrant, they dug up the entire garden but never found any money.

The anxious old man went to the prison on visiting day and told his son about the police, the search warrant and the digging. "Now what do I do," he asked his son.

His son smiled and said, "Go ahead and plant your potatoes. It's the best I could do for you from here."

Where do you turn when you need creative help?

I worked for a group of professors who studied health economics at a large, Midwestern research university just a year prior to the Hillary-goes-to-Washington-to-change-health-care time period. This group knew that they had good information to share based on solid research from well-respected researchers, but they didn't seem to be able to get it into the arena where it would have some impact. So, they hired me to "get the word out."

S.M.H 1949 ♀ 弖

Successfully attempting to stray as little as possible from the humanities in college, I got a shaky B in Econ 101 but never really felt I understood anything. I believed either economics was so difficult I couldn't grasp it or economics was so simple that they embellished it, thus masking its simplicity. At the time, I believed the former, but I learned it was closer to the latter while in my role at the university. Before I could write about the research, I had to get smarter about economics. They knew economics; I had to learn. Once my colleagues realized how simple they had to make this for me, we all relaxed and enjoyed our journey.

They taught me economic theories with food.

Beginning my lessons, one professor asked me how much I would spend for a banana. I said I would pay around 25 cents. He then asked me how much I would pay for a second banana. I thought probably 25 cents. What if you wanted to buy 20 bananas? Less than 25 cents. How about 1,000 bananas? Much less. So I learned the theory of supply and demand.

We examined how long it took for the free food that people put in the break room at the office to disappear. This might be the birthday cake you didn't want to have at

> Get out of your own head once in awhile. Sometimes it isn't too pretty in there.
>
> J.G. 1949 ♂

111

home because of the calories, the Girl Scout cookies you were bullied into buying or the two box lunches not eaten at the meeting the day before always short the cookies. The questions included: Did it matter if the food was old or not? Did it matter that the food was appetizing or not? Did it matter that it was the only food in the break room? The list went on, and I learned about the theory of rational choice.

My confidence grew, so cashing in on my newfound understanding of economics at the next staff meeting; I suggested a new vehicle to report their research findings. To provide an example, I studied a complicated health services research study, mocked up a one-page overview of what I thought to be its most vital information and put it in everyday English. To my chagrin, the professors were shocked and not in a good way. In their eyes, I had dumbed down their work. After much cajoling from me, they agreed to start a pilot series of one-page research project overviews *as long as I didn't send it to any of their colleagues.* I agreed and began the pilot.

Here comes the punch line. One day, one of the professors who was particularly resistant to the one-page research report came into my office saying that he had just gotten a call from one of the national gurus of health economics who wanted for more information on the study he had read about in the one-page research report. Needless to say, the mailing list was expanded to all of their colleagues, and my credibility as a communicator soared. Because my view of the world was different from theirs, they saw things differently.

We tend to see the world though our own lens of experience, and it sometimes takes something outside our understanding to create a personal revolution. This something outside our understanding can be other people's points of view, and for this reason, every individual committed to finding the person they were intended to be needs to choose and use a personal board of directors. Choosing a personal board of directors harnesses the power of other pieces of the puzzle that the cooperative universe provides.

If chosen wisely, your personal board of directors certainly will allow you access to other points of view and wisdom others have learned along the way. If chosen wisely, this group provides both wisdom and support for you to become the person you were intended to be. They will support what you need and want to create in your life. They can hold up a mirror for you to see clearly who you are, challenge you to think out of the box about who you could become and help you discover vehicles to get you there.

> Be open to others and to the idea that someone else might like you and want to spend time with you. Don't be so prickly.
> K.A. 1962 ♀

> Accept help when you need it.
> K.A. 1962 ♀

As you begin to think about the people you would like on this board, there are five things to consider:

> Think big and set bold goals. You will attract people who also think big and set bold goals.
>
> J.W. 1967 ♂

1. Choose advisers that have your benefit in mind. Several of my board of directors read the early drafts of this book. One of them suggested that an important part of choosing people for a personal board of directors was that they love you.
2. Think of this team as the people who you know well and are easy for you to call and ask, "What do you think?"
3. Choose advisers that you can think of as your Darwin or your Einstein. The development of Darwin's theory of evolution by natural selection turned the way we thought about the world on its head. In the same way, even though we may not all understand Einstein's $E=MC^2$, most acknowledge that it completely changed our worldview. You need people who will challenge your thinking in the same way. For your board of directors, this often means people that are different from you in some way — different career, different upbringing or different life choices.
4. Choose advisers with whom you can have a healthy give-and-take. Think of people who will respectfully listen to your ideas but are capable of respectfully disagreeing with you. You must be willing to listen to your advisers, so choose peo-

ple that you respect enough to hear out their ideas. After all, they will only be as effective as you allow them to be.

5. Revisit your criteria for board membership after you have completed reading this book, and then consider whether there are areas of expertise you need in your advisers. If you have decided you need to work on certain areas of your life, consider who might be able to give you another perspective on that area. Do you need someone who is a great networker? Do you need someone who has established a spiritual practice you admire? Do you need someone who works independently? You get the idea.

Decide what you need from your board and how you will get it from them. Once you have thought of four or five people, meet with them individually and invite them to join your personal board. Let them know why you chose them specifically using the list above. Be clear about what you are asking them to do for you. People are more likely to agree to a defined period of time, so tell them this is a one-year commitment, and, if you need them longer, discuss that later. Let them know how often you will meet, or if you plan to call them whenever needed or only quarterly. Decide what specifically you want from them. Consider having a kickoff meeting at your home over dinner. At least one meeting with everyone in the

> Free advice is not worth the price.
>
> O.D. 1950 ♂

same room will open the door to their working together synergistically.

> Lighten up! Don't feel you need to convince everyone why you are doing what you are doing. Use your sense of humor to diffuse difficult situations. Don't make life harder than it needs to be.
>
> M.R. 1970 ♂

S.M.H 1949 ♀ ䷓

Notes to Self for Chapter Ten

Want to work on the ideas in this chapter further? Deep Dive Exercises for Chapter Ten are on Page 231.

Chapter Eleven

Snap: Four Steps to Self-Transformation

When my son was in third grade he convinced me to enroll him in karate class. The first few months of the class involved learning steps and routines, but soon the instructor said they were going to begin to learn contact: punching, jabbing and slamming. I was horrified and told the instructor that my little angel of a son would never be able to hit another person. The instructor responded, "Everyone is different, but watch when he makes his first hit. If he leans backward, he doesn't like it and never will; if he learns forward, he likes it and always will." My angel leaned forward.

S.M.H 1949 ♀ 冨

When people ask what this book is about, I have several talking point options depending on the audience. Sometimes I say it is about why I got a tattoo, sometimes I say it is about changes I made to my life when I turned 60 and often I say it is about how I intentionally transformed. At some point, I can see people either lean back or lean forward when I say *self-transformation*. If they lean forward, they then ask how I managed to do it. I now see it took four things:

1. A strong desire to transform;
2. A belief that people can transform;
3. A belief that good turning point should never be wasted; and
4. A willingness to let change happen.

> Regrets arise more from the things you don't do than from the things you do. Take action —try to be more comfortable with slightly more risk than none at all. Say yes more often to people and activities.
>
> K.A. 1962♀

You can use these tools to support the changes that lead to your self-transformation. Let's look at each separately.

1. A strong desire to transform: Once I saw myself as a child of the universe born for a unique and vital purpose, the importance of transforming became clear and compelling. Remember Ralph in Chapter Two? Knowing that my piece of the puzzle involved helping other people like Ralph transform in order to fulfill their unique role gave me a strong desire to transform. I felt the importance and a responsibility to the puzzle; I longed to fulfill my role it.

119

> Take action —
> try to be more comfortable with slightly more risk than none at all.
>
> E.G. 1947 ♂

Your sense of importance may come from the acknowledgement that *where you are* and *what you are* isn't right. Think of your life now, then take your age, add the number of years you have left until your average life expectancy, and decide if you can live as you are for that number of years. Or does something need to change? At age 60, with an average life expectancy of 87, I would have 27 more years of living as I have been. That seemed intolerable and made this important for me. What gives you a strong desire to transform?

Sharks need to be in constant forward motion to survive; they are in motion even when asleep. In the same way, the opposite of transformation is not merely staying in the same place; the opposite of transformation is drowning. Do you think you are figuratively drowning in some way? You could be drowning in debt, drowning in drugs, drowning in apathy, drowning in depression, drowning in fear, drowning in bad relationships. Lots of ways to drown.

Or, think of the boiling frog story with the premise that if a frog is placed in boiling water, it will jump out, but if it is placed in cold water that is slowly heated, it will not perceive the danger and will be cooked to death. Would you know if the temperature of your water was increasing?

S.M.H 1949 ♀ 冨

If you are drowning, the next question you need to ask yourself is —can you learn how to swim? Remember the cooperative universe is ready to help, and your subconscious brain can be reprogrammed.

When do your swimming lessons start?

2. A belief that people can transform: You now are beginning to feel the pull of transformation. The questions you have to ask yourself are simple: Is this the time you actively engage and support the longed for transition? Is this the time to be the person you were meant to be? Is this the time that you clearly see your puzzle piece and claim it? What is holding you back?

Most of us have had the desire for transformation at some time in our lives. We have had the desire to change jobs. We have had the desire to quit smoking. We have had the desire to go back to school. We have had the desire to be more confident. We have had the desire to be a better partner or better parent. The list is long.

> Never let the critics tell you who you are. And be especially aware of the inner critic that robs you of the joy in today.
>
> D.K. 1955 ♀

Once you know you can transform, transforming is simple. Knowing you can transform is the more difficult step. Once you know you can transform, the change happens quickly. How can you come to believe that transformation is possible?

If I were to write a letter to my younger self, I would share the two things I now know about change:

> - People are capable of change, but they will only do things that are important to them. This is why people who don't know how to swim sometimes find their way to shore. First they have to know they are drowning. Next they need to want to get to shore.
> - While everything resists change, it can happen quickly and at any time.
>
> S.M.H 1949♀

Let's look at my first piece of advice above. Consider whether your subconscious mind thinks that people are capable of change. If you think people can't change, then you won't be able to change yourself. If you need to change your thinking, find examples that support this philosophy; read biographies that support this idea. Use affirmations if needed. Remember what Henry Ford said, "If you think you can or think you can't, you are right."

> The future doesn't just happen – it is created.
>
> H.M. 1923♂

Do you believe in transformation? Here is a good affirmation to try:

S.M.H 1949 ♀ 彐

I am grateful I can make the changes I want and need in my life.

3. A belief that good turning point should never be wasted: If turning points can be a tool to help you on your journey, how can you help yourself make the turning point work for you?

Once I felt the urgency to transform and knew that I could, I didn't waste a perfectly good turning point. There are times when the things you barely see out of the peripheral vision of your memory come into full focus; times when you fully see the reality of your life. Moments of clarity. Deciding the shape of my tattoo was one of my turning points. Actually getting the tattoo was mere confirmation of this fact. Marking it with a tattoo helped. Marking it in some other significant way will work. Wear a bracelet on your wrist as a reminder of the turning point. Put a daily tickler on our electronic calendar to remind you of the turning point. I didn't forget this perfectly good turning point. Mark the occasion so you don't waste your next turning point—so it does become just another crisis to be endured.

> Nurture a forward-thinking attitude. Have gratitude for what your life is and is becoming.
>
> R.M. 1966♀

Historically, such turning point moments could be either a slow realization or a sudden flash of insight. No matter what the initial speed was, I never allowed them to stay. I never paid attention to them. I wasted them. Not consciously, of course. Fog loves fog. And fog begets fog.

This time was different. Although I am sure I thought each revelation I had was also different at the time, somehow I knew on a cellular level that this one was on to which I needed to pay attention. Knowing that a turning point could be a powerful tool, I used it.

The cooperative universe wants us to learn our lessons on the journey, so it provides nudges. Nudges start with a tap on the back, and if the lessons aren't learned, the nudges escalate. A slap on the back, a bop on the head, a two-by-four between the eyes. Perhaps I had gotten enough two-by-fours. Perhaps it was the fact I was nearing my sixtieth year. Perhaps it was because not seeing them became harder to manage. Sometimes fog lifts unexpectedly.

Historically, such moments also produced resolve in me. Fleeting, but resolve just the same, as in *this time I am going to get my life in order; this time I will hold on to what is; so I can move to what I want it to be; this time I am going to get it done*.

This resolve was frequently documented, adding insult to injury. In my thirties, just such a moment prompted me to

> Be ready to admit a situation is not working instead of trying to fix it. It's ok to say that something doesn't work for you and move on instead of trying forever to make it ok or justify why you should stick with it.
>
> B.B. 1926 ♂

> Believe there is a reason for everything.
>
> D.H. 1922 ♀

journal that the steering wheel of my life was in front of me and mine for the taking. This insight was followed by a commitment to put my hands on the steering wheel and start driving. I'm not sure how long that one lasted, but I do know the rest of the journal is blank.

> Doing nothing is doing something.
>
> J.W. 1967 ♂

I still believe all of these turning point moments were "Eurekas!" or most certainly "Eureka-like". They just weren't durable. None of them were. The irony is it was precisely during one such moment I realized the problem was not that I didn't have such moments, but rather that I lost them so quickly. Lost, of course, sounds like it was out of my control, like when you lose your car keys but you know they are around here somewhere. These were more like having lost the keys, and not even knowing what keys were.

The conscious mind and the unconscious mind were at work. Something in that my subconscious mind created the belief that I couldn't transform. I acted on the belief I created. This time I created another belief on which to act. Here is an affirmation to use:

> *This turning point will be the beginning of the changes I will make in my life.*

Turning points are a tool to help you on your journey. Below is a step to help you get to your turning point:

4. A willingness to let change happen: I desired transformation, believed I could transform and so far, had a good un-wasted turning point. Now what? The next question I asked was - am I capable of change? I want transformation, but am I willing to do what it takes to transform.

> Remember that you can change your mind.
>
> H.M. 1927 ♂

The second piece of advice to my younger self, *While everything resists change, it can happen quickly and at any time*, stems from the tracks in my snow left by Thomas Kuhn's landmark book on the history of science, *The Structure of Scientific Revolutions.*[xii] While many of us think of science as discovering new and never thought of before ideas, Kuhn writes that one goal of science is to find models that will account for as many observations as possible *within* a coherent framework. Just as most of us want to maintain the status quo, so too do scientists. Usually this coherent framework is the prevailing scientific thought about our world. So, scientists do research and most often that research confirms what we already know further proving that what we "know" is true.

Once in awhile, a scientist comes up with something that doesn't fit prevailing scientific thought. Initially, such a discovery isn't welcomed because it may mean what has gone before is wrong.

S.M.H 1949 ♀ 畐

Take Nicolas Copernicus whose 1543 book, *On the Revolutions of the Heavenly Spheres,* presented the idea that the earth revolved around the Sun. This idea was the opposite of the prevailing idea that the earth was the center of the universe, and everything revolved around the earth. His idea didn't fit the prevailing world theory, and scientists resisted it. Enter Galileo. Using the first astronomical telescope to support his work, in 1632 he published *Dialogue Concerning the Two Chief World Systems*, which confirmed Copernicus was right. Not quite ready for the scientific revolution, the church brought Galileo before the Inquisition and made him renounce all his beliefs and writings supporting the Copernican theory.

> When you go to Harvard, you get used to things being complicated. Don't think that some things are too simple to be effective.
>
> D.K. 1920♀

In other words, everything resists change. And shifts do not occur often or easily.

Kuhn wrote that science can undergo revolutions, also called "paradigm shifts," during which the basic nature a particular scientific field is abruptly transformed. This, however, usually doesn't happen until the new idea doesn't fit the old mold many times.

In other words, after more and more scientists found more and more situations that didn't fit the flat world theory, they began to believe that Galileo was right. When

> As hokey as it may sound, follow your own feelings and what you know to be true. You don't have to follow a crowd to be happy.
>
> K.A. 1962 ♀

the idea of a round world caught on, science changed quickly and all the textbooks were re-written.

Once the new paradigm is established as truth, scientists return to normal science, solving problems that confirm the new paradigm and resisting problems that create solutions that do not fit the prevailing mode—until the next paradigm shift.

What does this have to do with finding and becoming the person you were intended to be? If you are a teacher who dreams of being a painter, your prevailing scientific theory is about being a teacher. If you are unhappy in your job, you think of teaching at a different school rather than teaching something completely different or leaving the profession all together. You resist changing your existing theory. Something dramatic needs to happen to cause a paradigm shift from teacher to painter.

When I read Kuhn, I thought of bending a branch until it broke. The tension in the wood right before it cracks is something familiar to all of us. If you can't imagine that tension right before the crack —go find a twig and try it. It takes the right amount of pressure at the right place to get the branch to crack. And, if you stop right before it does break, it can go back to being the branch it was before.

What would it take to break your branch? What would it take to make you see that you are a person who was born to be a good friend, when right now you have only acquaintances? What would it take for you to see yourself as brave enough to go on a world tour by yourself when you have never traveled outside the state? What would it take for you to see that you were meant to impact the way we teach kids when you haven't been in school since graduation?

Goethe spoke of commitment and the impact it can have. If you have had your turning point, your next step is to make a commitment. Not a wish nor a hope, but a commitment.

If you are truly committed, you say, "I will do whatever is necessary to make my goal of claiming my piece of the puzzle achievable this year," rather than, "I want to find my unique piece of the puzzle."

Notice the difference? If you own your mental position and know you can control it, you become the most powerful force in your life. Then the cooperative universe kicks in, too. The good news is, only you control your life. The bad news, being in control of your life means you

> Be authentic.
> T.L.1965♀

and you alone must claim responsibility for both success and failure.

Take me. It wasn't my fault my parents raised me to be a princess and didn't want me to worry my pretty little head about money. They never taught me about money, but it is my responsibility to learn how to manage money now. It isn't my fault I was raised from good alcoholic stock and have a propensity to over drink, but it was my responsibility to stop drinking now.

I was the only one who could do those things. I was the only thing stopping me from doing them.

It took years on my journey to be able to synthesize my experience and be clear about my ability to find my piece of the puzzle. There were numerous starts and stops. At the beginning of my 60th year, I decided to commit to conscious support of my journey. The cooperative universe kicked in.

At the end of 60th and transformational year, noticing people noticed my transformation and asked me about my turning point. Was there a specific precipitating event? And, at the bottom of all of these questions was the question they really wanted me to answer: How can I get to my turning point?

While deciding what shape my tattoo would take was certainly the impetus to review my life, and my conversation with Ralph gave focus, I think it is fair to say the answer to the precipitating event question is no and yes.

No, because there was nothing that hadn't happened many times before. I had failed to complete a book many times. I had woken up many times after too much to drink the night before with new resolve to quit. I had been disappointed by people close to me many times and punished both of us for that. I had robbed Peter to pay Paul many times with credit cards.

I looked at my looming 60th birthday and felt I could well be living this same way for the next 40 years. The idea sickened me, and something in me changed. I felt the discrepancy of what I was and what I wanted to be. I wanted something different. I wanted to be authentic.

My twig broke.

I had believed for many years the supportive universe had something in mind for me, but I also believed I had missed my chance. I knew from tracks in the snow I had many nudges and opportunities I ignored, missed or squandered. I believed it could have worked but that it was too late. I bought into the possibilities but told myself I had come to the party too late.

For many years of my life, I was in therapy, and it was a vital part of my journey. I now see my therapist perhaps once or twice a year for a tune-up and oil change. When I said to her for perhaps the hundredth time, "I just have this feeling that if things in my family of origin had been different, I would have been something different. Like President of the United States or something," she said, "If that is what you really want, what is stopping you from doing that now?"

It was an *"Aha"* moment, and when Ralph told me it was too late for him, I heard my voice. She was right. My parents were no longer living. I had worked though my demons. I —it turns out —was the only thing standing in my way.

> Do your best as you see it.
>
> C.A.1922 ♂

If you are taking notes for the quiz, I am going to repeat that one: I was the only thing standing in my way.

If I had to identify a turning point, it was the moment I realized that I was responsible for myself and my journey, and I was the only thing standing in my way. I felt *self-efficacy* – I believed in my ability to accomplish a task by my own effort.

Swami Vivekenanda, the man often said to have introduced Hinduism to the modern Western culture, believed that just as certain world religions say people who do not believe in a personal God outside themselves are atheists, those of the Hindu religion say a person who does not believe in himself is an atheist. Vivekenanda felt that not believing in the splendor of one's own soul is atheism.[xiii]

My strong desire to transform, my belief that I could transform, my well used turning point, and my broken twig all came when I began to believe in the splendor of my own soul.

Notes to Self for Chapter Eleven

Want to work on the ideas in this chapter further? Deep Dive Exercises for Chapter Eleven are on Page 233.

S.M.H 1949 ♀ 금

Chapter Twelve

Get to *"just do it"*: Motivation

Once upon a time there were two warring tribes. One lived in the lowlands and the other high in the mountains. One day the mountain people invaded the lowland people, and besides taking food and goods, they also kidnapped a lowland baby and took the infant back up to the mountains.

Even though the lowland people didn't know how to climb the mountain, they sent out a group of strong and able lowland men to climb the mountain and bring the baby home.

The men tried one method of climbing after another. They tried one trail after another. But after several days, they had climbed only several hundred feet from where they had started. Feeling hopeless, the lowland men gave up and prepared to return to their village below.

As they were packing up their gear to return home, they saw the baby's mother walking toward them coming down the mountain with the baby strapped to her back.

One man greeted her and said, "How did you climb this mountain when we, the strongest and most able men in the village, couldn't?"

The mother just shrugged her shoulders and said, "It isn't your baby."

We all desire to become what we are capable of becoming, and there are consequences if that mission is not accomplished. Aristotle believed happiness is the meaning and the purpose of life and that a person can find happiness only by using all of his abilities and capabilities.[xiv] For Aristotle, the consequence of not using all your gifts would be an unhappy life.

> Stand up for yourself. Know who that self is. Speak up!
>
> **O.A.1920♀**

People ask me what was different about my motivation during my transformational year. Why was different this time?

First, I considered the consequence of not being my destined self: not being at peace with myself. I was no longer willing to accept this consequence. I was motivated because I knew that not being at peace with myself and leading an unhappy, unfulfilled life was no longer an option for me.

Abraham Maslow, an American psychologist and founder of humanistic psychology, goes further when he said, "What a man can be, he must be. A musician must make music, an artist must paint, a poet must write, if he is to be ultimately at peace with himself."[xv]

Must is a strong word. We need to be who we are meant to be in the same way we must have food and water. This longing to be who you can be is primal. It is vital. Without it, or without being on the conscious journey towards it, we die. It may not be literal death, but certainly a psychological and spiritual death. One of our Voices of Wisdom said something similar:

> Don't let your father tell you not to be an architect. He wasn't born to be an architect —you were.
>
> B.J. 1975 ♂

I often hear things from people that give me a glimpse into the person they were meant to be. I give you two powerful examples:

- One friend, who had a successful career in communications with an insurance company, always talked about disliking her job because it didn't make a difference. When I got to know her better, she shared with me that right out of graduate school —where she studied health communications—she turned down an offer to work on a new TV concept called *Sesame Street*. She would have worked on the team that developed material to support good health habits in pre-school children. Instead of taking the job, she decided to marry and move away from New York to a city where his job took them. Where might she look to find her piece of the puzzle?
- My mother graduated from college when most women didn't even have the opportunity to attend and was beginning a promising career at General Mills, when World War Two began. This spunky girl from North Dakota quit her job and joined the OSS (the organization that became the CIA) as a civilian. She lived in London during the Blitz and was personally responsible for listening to the members of the Jedburg teams that were dropped behind enemy lines for reconnaissance.

When and if they returned, she wrote their stories. As with many of her generation, she married after the war and became a housewife. While resigned to this role, she was unhappy most of her life. When I moved her out of her house into a senior living condo, my daughter came across an old box full of things the Jedburg team members had brought her years earlier. This prompted a very long and lively afternoon of stories about her experience during the war. I will never forget the wistful look on my mother's face when my daughter found a book about the Jedburg teams and gave it to her grandma, saying, "You should have written this. Your stories are better." What was she born to do?

To quote Maslow again, "What a man can be, he must be. A musician must make music, an artist must paint, a poet must write, if he is to be ultimately at peace with himself." [xvi]

Finding your destined, authentic self is not optional or extra credit. Knowing this allows you to make the commitment. Making the commitment gives you the motivation.

The second thing different was that this time I knew that I —and I alone —was responsible for making something

> Don't give up on things that are tough. You sometimes want an easy answer when there isn't one. Accept that some things are tough and get on with it —you will figure it out.
>
> K.A. 1962 ♀

happen. And, I was completely committed to making it happen. This commitment was reinforced with the knowledge that I had the power to make it happen. And the cooperative universe was going to kick in to help me. I felt unstoppable.

As I looked clearly at what I wanted to create in my life, what I needed to myself rid of became obvious. I needed time at night to write, so I needed to quit drinking at night. If I was going to publish this book, I needed to have enough money to do just that, so I needed to understand money, and have enough left over to publish this book. If I were going to focus on my journey and this book, I needed to stop focusing on others and focus on my writing.

So no one event, but rather many repeat events led me to decide that I deserved to be the person I was meant to be and that the universe deserved my being that person, too.

> Say yes more often to people and activities.
>
> K.A. 1962♀

Third, I realized no amount of *if onlys* could stop me from being that person. Once I realized those two things, the immortal words of Nike commercials kicked in: *"Just do it."*

I got a tattoo to mark my commitment to transform, and then I "just did it".

Here are the six ways of thinking to support you in *just doing it*.

1. Know that you have a unique role to play in the world; this is important and even vital work. Your piece in the puzzle is important to you and to the puzzle. Feel the importance of your transformation.
2. Know it is never too late to play your role—age is not a factor. Instead of wishing you would have done something earlier, do something in the only time you can — now. Feel the rush of starting over.
3. Know that the cooperative universe wants you to find your piece of the puzzle and will support you. Believe Goethe when he said once you are truly committed to this goal, "All manner of unforeseen incidents and meetings and material assistance, which no man could have dreamed would (have) come," will come your way. Begin to experience the assistance.
4. Use affirmations, positive self-talk and personal talking points to firmly plant these six ideas in your head, and form a personal board of directors to keep on track.

5. Make it real by telling a few trusted friends. I want to reinforce the *few* part of this statement by sharing my experience. I am blessed with a great network and many wonderful friends with whom I share almost everything. Please note the *almost* in the last statement. There were a few things I shared with no one, and this list should look familiar. I didn't share my concerns with money and drinking. I didn't share the level of my frustration with my writing or the problems my expectations of others caused. The things that were causing me to feel the most disconnected from my authentic self were precisely the things that I hadn't previously share. This time was different. I authentically shared my biggest challenges with a few friends. And, to reinforce how good I was at being unauthentic, all were surprised at all four of these areas of concern. The authenticity of sharing is a big step towards becoming the person you want to be.
6. Remember the words of the philosopher Soren Kierkegaard, "Face the facts of being what you are, for that is what changes what you are." [xvii] Know who you are and know that it will change you.

With this commitment, my good feelings about myself and my journey grew. Once I knew that my puzzle piece was writing this book, it was easier to determine things getting the way of accomplishing that – interactions with others, drinking and money worries.

I told some trusted people what I was doing to make it real and then:

- Instead of wanting others to change in the way I believed they should, I stopped having expectations of them. I decided to allow the cooperative universe to help them on their journey instead of me.
- Instead of worrying and wishing about my finances, I set up a system to track what was happening with the money in my control and updated my system every month.
- Instead of thinking I may be drinking too much and too often, I stopped drinking.
- Instead of writing one third of a book every few years, I made a commitment to complete this book before I turned 61 and wrote it.

In the final analysis, what was different this time was my commitment. I clearly saw the goal and kept my eye on it. While hundreds, perhaps thousands of books have been written on what motivates people, I think the simplicity of the Nike slogan captures it all: "*Just do it*". Sometimes simple things are best.

In her books, *Thin for Life*[xviii] and, *Sober for Good*[xix], author Anne Fletcher identified and interviewed people who either successfully lost and kept weight off or quit drinking for more than five years. After reading both books, I saw a similar simplicity to their success. They reported:

- The old way of living—either drinking too much or weighing too much —was simply was no longer an option for them,

- They shunned complexity and made a simple decision to eat differently or quit drinking permanently, and

- While they used outside resources, they created a plan or program that was uniquely their own.

Notice the commitment in each of these statements. Notice the simplicity. Notice they were their own best advice givers.

"Just do it." And, then the cooperative universe will kick in.

There are four steps to help get to *"just do it"*:

1. Have a goal clearly in your mind. An elevator speech would be best. You can use it as an af-

firmation to mold your thinking, and you can use it as a personal talking point to let others quickly know what you are doing and why. They will help with your upward spiral. I would suggest something like the following:

> *My goal is to enjoy the journey to claim my piece of the puzzle. I know once I claim it, I will claim my peace in the puzzle.*

Or, if your goal is clearer:

> *My goal is to have my travel business successfully in place by the end of this year.*

2. Commit to your goal. This means accepting your goal, taking complete responsibility for your goal yourself, and being willing to make any changes necessary to reach it. If you start feeling resentful, rebellious, or are beginning to blame forces outside yourself for being in the situation you're in, you probably are not yet fully committed. If you are fully committed, the cooperative universe will kick in. Feeling shaky? Look for nudges from the universe to guide you. Wavering? Use your elevator speech.

3. Have a plan, work your plan and stop daily to look carefully at what you've been doing that is working and what is not. Your board of directors

> Listen to that growing voice inside of you. Everyday you are learning who you are and who aren't. Pay attention to the direction you are being pointed. Listen to yourself and what you have learned.
>
> J.T. 1945 ♂

can help you with feedback. Or ask one member of your board to be your touch point perhaps by asking them if they would be open to receiving a daily update via email as to your progress. Be sure to be clear with them about the kind of response you desire from them.

4. Pay attention to your thoughts. Are they supporting your goal or not? Remember your mind believes what you tell it. Are you molding them and harnessing it with affirmations? When something happens, do you use your elevator speech or your talking points to reinforce what you are doing and why? To be completely responsible for all your reactions to people, places and things, you need to harness the power of your thoughts. Catch yourself thinking and be sure you approve of the messages.

5. Imagine how you will feel once you transform. Remind yourself of that feeling during your process.

What did this mean for me?

Every time I thought of having a drink, I reminded myself why I made the decision to stop. I would never finish this book if I were drinking every night, and I had to finish it. I visualized what I was like when I was drinking and what I was like not drinking. I would visualize how I would feel in the morning if I chose drinking over writing. I would often say to myself what a non-drinking friend shared with me, "I have never seen anyone or anything improve with a few drinks."

Every time I wanted to spend money I didn't have, I thought of the good feeling I had each time I reviewed my spreadsheet. If I needed motivation, I would get out my spreadsheet and review it. I would say the affirmation, "Everything I need I already have," as I drove to the store. My need to spend shrunk. I would often say the affirmation, "Every day in every way, I am getting better and better."

Every time expectations of another person led me to be angry and every time I began to feel I had an expectation about what another person did, I reflected on my growth during this transformational year. I thought about whether my expectations had ever changed anyone, and the answer was *no*. I would often say two affirmations, "It is easy for me to allow others to move successfully though their journey just as I move though mine," and "I trust that my loved one has the support of the cooperative universe just as I do." When I spoke to people, I listened more and talked less.

> Believe me when I tell you that you have power. YOU HAVE POWER! Use it to benefit you and to benefit me.
>
> E.E. 1940 ♀

Every time I doubted my ability to create this book, I examined where that thought came from, and it was usually from my subconscious brain telling me I never finished these things. I would readjust my thinking and also say the affirmation, "I am a beloved child of the cooperative universe and by writing this book, I am claiming my piece of the puzzle."

I know I have the power and ability to make a difference in my journey. I know I am a unique person with a unique journey. I know the cooperative universe is supporting me on my journey.

With this knowledge, I just did it.

Hopefully you are motivated and believe that your goal of finding your authentic self, and your place in the cooperative universe, is achievable. Not yet? Ask yourself these questions to find what might be getting in the way of your motivation.

Is transformation too big a word?

If transformation sounds like too big a word, use another word instead. Logical progression. Natural course of my life. Next indicated action. Choose words that make sense to you and that will move you along your journey.

> Others are watching, with wise eyes, and you aren't fooling anyone. Live a life that won't haunt you in your middle age, much less during the reflections of old age, should you live that long. As the saying goes, integrity is doing the right thing when no one else is looking.
>
> J.D. 1949♀

Are you afraid you won't get the steps right?

Just as you are unique, so is your process. There is no right way. What would it look like to believe you can influence the choices and circumstances in your life? Do them. Believe that they will be transformational. Believe that change is possible. The rest will follow. What we focus on grows. Focus on being the person you know you can be. What we practice, we get better at doing. Practice doing what it takes to be that person. Don't know what to practice? Do what you think you maybe should practice. If it isn't right, you'll get a nudge to help you get closer to what is right.

Feeling discouraged? Feel like giving up? Do you feel like even if your life isn't perfect, you don't need any help and will be just fine?

You may be defending yourself against possible failure by thinking these self-defeating thoughts. If you are to reach your full potential, try to reprogram your mental computer with these affirmations:

> *I am grateful to say yes to all that I am and all this life has to offer.*
>
> *I am grateful to fully realize that I deserve what I desire.*

Say these affirmations frequently for five days, and then look at your process and your commitment to it again.

Feel that you won't finish what you start?

Begin with small steps and watch them grow. An African saying asks how you eat an elephant. The answer — *one bite at a time*. Once you believe that you are a unique person in this cooperative universe, and through positive self-talk and affirmations you begin to like and accept yourself, your confidence will grow. A positive cycle begins. As your belief in your ability to impact your life grows, you become more confident. As your confidence grows, your desire to improve grows and you become more willing to risk trying something new and risking mistakes along the way. Experiencing success at some of the new things you try will support more trying. And, more success supports the idea your efforts bring forth improvements. Improvements to your life result in a feeling of control over your own life, and this develops into a stronger sense of responsibility to yourself. To come full circle, this stronger sense of responsibility to yourself supports your belief in your own ability to do so. Your have created a positive cycle of personal growth for yourself —one small step at a time.

Think you can't do it?

Be encouraged by the words of Henry David Thoreau:

> I know of no more encouraging fact than the unquestionable ability of man to elevate his life by conscious endeavor.

Know that you can reprogram your subconscious brain and begin to say affirmations like the following to reprogram it:

> *I have the ability to elevate my life by conscious endeavor; I know what those endeavors are and can easily and successfully perform them.*

Feel like you don't have support?

If you have made up your mind, know that you are not alone and your support is formidable. The cooperative universe is waiting patiently to be your partner.

Read this quotation by Johann Wolfgang von Goethe wrote aloud:

> Your intentions will assist you in taking greater control of your life. A working definition for intention is: "to have in mind a purpose or plan, to direct the mind, to aim." Lacking intention, we sometimes stray without meaning or direction. But with it, all the forces of the universe can align to make even the most impossible, possible. My intention is to transform the conversation around dreams from fear and doubt, to hope and possibility, followed by action and results.

Then close your eyes and visualize transformation.

Read aloud what Thoreau believed and believe in your *unquestionable ability to elevate your life by conscious endeavor.* Read aloud what Goethe wrote and believe that *all the forces of the universe can align to make even the most impossible, possible.* Close your eyes and feel the possibilities.

You already know what your life is like now. Can you see what your life would be like if you found your authentic self?

> Ask yourself often – if not now, when.
>
> L.R.1932 ♂

If not, use the tool of creative visualization. Creative visualization is an age-old technique that—like any skill—can be strengthened through regular practice, so this may take some practice. Let's say you are having trouble getting started on your plan. Visualizing what your life would be like following a transformation helps. Here is what you might do:

- Relax and close your eyes. Visualize yourself in a wonderful place where you are feeling calm and peaceful. Pick a place you love and know well so you can imagine yourself there in the future. See it clearly as if it were a colorful and vivid picture. Imagine you have achieved your goal and now know the role you were intended to play. Luxuriate in the glow of the good feeling you have.
- Recreate this image as often as possible until it becomes familiar.

- Once you are able to easily recreate this image and the feeling you have, extend your visualization.
- Imagine a wise and kindly man comes into the picture. You are not surprised to see him and welcome him into your picture. As your eyes meet, you know that he has information vital to your journey. He hands you a book and tells you everything will be made clear to you within the book.
- You thank him and hold the book close to your heart.
- You walk away and when you are ready, you open the book and read what is on the page. Read the words. They are exactly what you wanted to discover.

The first time I did this visualization, I opened the book and saw the words, "You can."

Open yourself up to the cooperative universe, where everything is possible, including finding the motivation you seek.

Notes to Self for Chapter Twelve

Want to work on the ideas in this chapter further? Deep Dive Exercises for Chapter Twelve are on Page 236.

Chapter Thirteen

Harness Your Resources: Needs and Wants

Once upon a time, there was a farmer who was dissatisfied with his lot in life. Urged on by his equally dissatisfied wife, he went to see the King to ask for a larger house.

"I work harder than any of my neighbors but still have a house smaller than any of them," he complained to the King. "Please give me the larger house—my wife and I deserve."

"Go home and bring your chickens into the house," said the King.

The dissatisfied farmer returned home and did just that.

A week later, he returned to the King and complained, "I now have the chickens in the house, and the house seems smaller than before."

"Go home and bring your cattle into the house," said the King.

The dissatisfied farmer returned home and did just that.

Five days later, he returned to the King and complained, "I now have the chickens and the cattle in the house and the house seems smaller than ever before. Please get me a larger house."

"Go home and bring your pigs into the house," said the King.

The dissatisfied farmer did just that.

After one day with chickens, cattle and pigs in the house, the dissatisfied farmer's wife said, "This is worse than before! We need a larger house more than ever before. Return to the King and ask for what we deserve."

The dissatisfied farmer returned to the King and said, "We can hardly find a place to stand in our house now with chickens, cattle and pigs, much less find a place to sleep. Please give us a larger house."

"Return home and take all the animals out of the house," said the King.

And, the dissatisfied farmer did just that and was dissatisfied no more because suddenly their house seemed spacious and they had all the room they needed, with room to spare.

During your journey to become your intended self, you will still have a job to go to, bills to pay and retirement for which to save. The cooperative universe provides the resources that you need to find and fulfill your piece of the puzzle, your job is to harness and utilize those resources. As with all things in your life, the resources you have and how you get those resources can be a tool to help or hinder you as you find your destined self. Knowing the difference between wants and needs will ensure that your resources support your journey. In the story above, the farmer and his wife confused what they wanted with what they needed. They were happy in the end, for even though the size of the house stayed the same, the farmer's perception of the size of his house changed.

> Material wealth does not matter. What matters is what we do with the wealth we have.
>
> J.W. 1967 ♂

Just like the farmer, each of us can change our perceptions about our resources. Remember, your brain doesn't evaluate data, it just takes it in. Just like the dissatisfied farmer, each of us can change our perceptions of what we have. But, instead of changing farm animals, we change the data we put in our brains.

In this chapter, you see how I consciously reprogrammed my subconscious mind to change my perception of my wants and my needs. You can do the same, and thereby, change your relationship with things like money, real estate, clothes, or vacations simply by using the tools provided in this book. You can also change your relationship with your job, which is how most of us get our resources. This chapter is divided into two parts, with a Notes to Self section following each part. The first part is about resources; the second is about your job.

Resources

I needed to change my relationship with money. Whatever it is that you feel you need more of —size of house, number of vacations, number of shoes—use my experience with money as an example. Substitute your own area of need/want confusion with the word *money* in this chapter.

Part of the transformation of my 60th year was changing my *perception* of money. I reprogrammed my brain to change my relationship with money, and in so doing, I learned to work with money rather than struggle against it. I began to experience abundance in my life. I came to believe that I had exactly what I needed.

My struggles with money were getting in the way of finding my piece of the puzzle. It was a distraction. It was a reason to not move forward. It was an excuse. I knew this from looking at my tracks in the snow.

When I was growing up in my parent's home, my parents were generous with money. I had plenty of it, but no control over it, and I worried about money. When I was a single parent in graduate school with no money, I worried about money. Then I was a stay-at-home mom married to a man with plenty of money, and I worried about money. When that man stopped having money and we

> I wished I had saved more money in high school.
>
> L.W. 1922 ♀

both had to scramble, I worried about money. When things got better and we both had good jobs, I worried about money.

From my tracks in the snow, I saw that I worried about money in every circumstance. It didn't matter whether I had money or not; I worried. This was not about money but about my *relationship* with money. And, since I believe that I am completely responsible to all my reactions to people, places and things, I knew I could do something about my reactions to and relationship with money.

Chapter Seven discussed the power of affirmations and positive self-talk as a tool for reprogramming our brains. Let me present the dark side of affirmations —negative self-talk. I call them "negfirmations" for they are the opposite of positive, uplifting affirmations. They are negative affirmations. If an affirmation declares that something is true and is a positive statement or judgment; negfirmations declare that a negative statement or judgment is true. Negfirmations shaped my relationship with money from an early age:

- My father grew up during the depression, at time when everything was uncertain and things were scarce. From him I learned – *There is not enough good stuff to go around. If you have more, I have less.*

- I have no doubt that my mother loved me, but she had difficulty expressing that love. She did so by buying me things. If I did something well, it would mean a trip to the clothing store. From her I learned —*Things make you happy.*
- After my father's death, my brother shared with me that our father had asked him to be sure I had enough money but not enough to make me independent. Unspoken norms are very strong in any family, and having grown up with this concept firmly and continually planted in the brain, I learned — *Money is complicated, so don't worry your pretty little head over it. You need someone to take care of you.*
- Until recently, I did not manage any money but gave that power to someone. From this I learned — *While I seem to have enough money, I never know if I will have enough tomorrow or the next day.*

These negfirmations were firmly planted, and just as I did with my plants, I watered them unconsciously everyday. And they grew. Because of these three negfirmations, I:

> Be more for others than your own success. It will come back to you.
>
> **D.H.P 1979 ♀**

- Resented the successes of others and envied their good fortune because I knew that if they had some there was less for me,
- Felt unloved and unlovable if I didn't have enough money,
- Believed that I wasn't smart enough to understand money, and
- Knew that I couldn't count on having money tomorrow even if I had some today.

In my 30s, when my husband's family company filed for bankruptcy, I unconsciously and consciously began saying — *I'll never have enough money again.* And, one day I realized that it sounded vaguely similar to the powerful affirmation I had said earlier *I have more than enough time to do all the things I want and need to do.*

Desperate, I started to say:

> *I have more than enough money to do all the things I want and need to do.*

My programming was so strong that I found I couldn't remember this simple phrase, so I wrote it on a piece of paper and carried with me everywhere.

While I began to feel more confident, I continued to unconsciously say the negfirmations at the same time, too. The old programming remained strong.

> Don't assume the people who spend a lot of money have a lot of money. You can only assume they spend a lot of money.
>
> J.C. 1965 ♂

S.M.H 1949 ♀ ䷀

A friend suggested I start thinking about abundance. I found the word itself unfamiliar. She suggested that abundance means having exactly what you need all the time, and suggested the following affirmations:

- *Money is good, and I enjoy having money.*
- *Money flows into my life easily.*
- *Everyday my bank balance is more than that of the previous day.*
- *I am a money magnet and attract money continuously.*
- *I am getting more and more prosperous day by day.*
- *I enjoy having abundance in my life.*

I began to change my thinking.

I next turned to my personal talking points and asked: What do I believe or hope to believe about having money? The result was Personal Talking Points Numbers Nine and Ten:

Personal Talking Point Number Nine: People can have secondary greatness or social recognition, and not have primary greatness, or goodness in their character. Therefore, I will remember that being is more important than having.

Personal Talking Point Number Ten: There is more than enough good stuff to go around; therefore, I will delight in the success of others as well as my own.

> When you compare yourself to others, please think more or people being in a circle rather than being on a ladder. No one above or below — all on the same level at different places.
>
> M.H. 1970 ♂

The first personal talking point reinforced the idea that whether I did or didn't have money or I didn't have money, I was still a good person. I stopped feeling bad about myself and my circumstances. The second allowed me to enjoy the abundance of others, allowing me to stop being jealous. Feeling bad about myself and my circumstances and being jealous of others were not only toxic; they took a lot of time. Once I was done with them, I could devote that time elsewhere.

I was transforming my relationship with money. But it wasn't until I set up a spreadsheet and tracked my monthly income, expenses and investments that I was able to stop money from getting in my way. I documented my progress and began a positive, upward spiral. My perception of *normal* began to shift to include new circumstances, habits and behaviors.

In this positive spiral, I began to consider the difference between what I wanted and what I needed.

In an effort to think differently, I got out some of my old college sociology class notes and found that one of traits that allowed humans to evolve is our adaptability. We acclimate to new situations quickly. If we apply this trait to happiness, the results suggest that *things* cannot make us happy in the long term precisely because we adapt to having them quickly. For example, we may be convinced that a new car will make us happy, and we will no doubt initially feel happy with the new car. But, because we are adaptable, we quickly acclimate to having it, and it no longer makes us happy. The car becomes another baseline, and we begin to look for something else that will make us happy. This would suggest that only experiences provide long lasting happiness, because we don't acclimate to the memory of a positive experience. We do not acclimate to a happy memory, so experiences like fishing with grandchildren, wonderful conversations with friends over dinner or finishing a marathon all continue to bring happiness because we cannot acclimate to them. They are a static point in time.

This is reinforced by a systematic study of 22 people who won major lotteries. Despite more money, each reverted to their original baseline level of happiness over time, winding up no happier than 22 matched controls. [xx]

So knowing that more money will not necessarily make me happy, and it is experiences not things that can make me happy, I began to think about my things. Here is what happened:

> Question your certainty. I have come to believe that "Opinions too strongly held are like earplugs; they allow you to hear only your own voice." Accept who you are and don't take yourself so damn seriously!
>
> K.A. 1951 ♀

- I began to actively seek out experiences and thoroughly enjoy them. If possible, I acquired

- something —a stone picked up on the wonderful walk on the beach, a photo of my grandchild sleeping in my arms —that helped me continue to treasure that moment.
- When I felt I needed to buy something, I tried to think about whether it was a *want-to-have* or a *need-to-have* item. If it were a *want-to-have*, I would first decide if I already had something like it that I could use instead. I made it a game to see how creative I could get finding something that would work. If I did find something, I didn't buy. I also thought about how I would feel about the purchase in a month. If it was a need, I actively bought things that I thoroughly liked and bought the best quality I could so the purchase would last.

Having enough money is necessary for survival, but just *how much is enough* seems to be the important question as we look at our peace in the puzzle. And we can control whether or not we feel abundance in our lives or not.

Feeling prosperous?

S.M.H 1949 ♀ 冨

Notes to Self for Resources

Want to work on the ideas in this chapter further? Deep Dive Exercises for Chapter Thirteen: Resources are on Page 238.

Job

Once you are clearer on what your needs are, you can consider your job, for it is how you get the resources to pay for what you need. Your job can be a tool to help or hinder your progress to discover your intended self. Your job can be a tool to help you find your piece of the puzzle only if you are clear on what you want your job to do for you. Consider the following story:

> Pay attention to aptitude tests. Then take a risk and push yourself in that direction.
>
> R.K. 1939 ♂

Faced with many employee disability claims caused by repetitive motion, a large clothing manufacturer contracted with an occupational therapist to see if something could be done to reduce injuries.

As the occupational therapist watched each employee do their small part to create children's denim overalls on the assembly line, she became puzzled as to how several employees seemed to genuinely enjoy the work even though they were doing the same thing over and over and over, only to do the same the next day.

One elderly lady in particular, whose job was to sew the top part of a latch on the left shoulder strap, fascinated her. How could she be smiling doing such repetitive and boring work? The occupational therapist's confu-

sion grew when she learned that this worker had done the same job for over 20 years.

One day as she watched the elderly woman reach into a bin of half competed overalls, take one out, reach into a box and take out the top part of the latch, expertly fold the strap over the latch and sew it in place before putting the still incomplete overalls in yet another bin. She became spellbound by the enthusiasm of the elderly woman and the smile on her face.

The occupational therapist knew she herself could never perform such work for more than a day much less perform it for over 20 years with a smile on her face. She needed to know she was contributing to some greater good, and she could not see any greater good in the left shoulder strap of a child's overalls.

The occupational therapist finally asked the old woman why she loved her job so much.

Without missing a stitch or a motion, the elderly woman responded, "This job has bought my house, helped all of my children get though college, buys gifts for my grandchildren and is helping me save for retirement. As I work, I imagine how much this job has helped my family."

Her job was not work. It was a blessing.

Like many people, I have had many jobs. I taught school, consulted with people about their parenting skills, found ways to reach out to women without jobs or resources, supported the communications and marketing of several organizations, translated healthcare ideas for the lay reader, established a corporate community relations department and supported people's philanthropy. I have enjoyed some of these jobs more than others. I felt I was accomplishing more in some of these jobs than others. I performed some of these jobs only because I needed the money or the benefits. However, each of these jobs gave me glimpses into my piece of the puzzle. Each was a nudge from the universe to become my destined self. Each job served a purpose, even though I was not clear what that purpose was at the time.

> If you love what you do for work, you'll never work a day in your life.
>
> R.K.1939 ♂

In the opening story, was the elderly woman's piece of the puzzle her expertise in sewing the left side of a child's overall or helping her family? Or was it her piece of the puzzle to live a life of gratitude? It could be either. Only she gets to decide. It is clear that the importance of the elderly woman's work was not *what* she did but *how and why* she did it.

Your job can be a tool for your transformation. There are several questions you need to ask yourself: Why do you do the work you do? What do you want your work to do for you? Money, prestige, a framework for your day, freedom, meaning, performing the work you are intended to do in the puzzle—there could be many possible answers.

I was once privileged to visit an 88-year-old woman in an assisted living facility. When I asked her if she liked where she was living, she shared with me the following:

> It took a little getting used to but eventually I started to enjoy all the activities they made available. But, over time, I felt myself getting depressed, so I talked to my doctor. The antidepressants helped but what helped more was my realizing that while I was busy, I wasn't purposeful. So, I started the quilting group, and now we send two quilts a year to soldiers. I feel much better.

On some level, she knew she was intended to help others. Even at 88, she needed to continue to help others to be at peace.

Again the question is, "What do you want your job to do for you?"

Peace in the Puzzle: Becoming Your Intended Self

Answer the question thoughtfully. In the 50s, many men found their identity in their jobs, and as a wise man said to me once as he looked at retirement, "If what you do is who you are, then when you don't you aren't."

Your work may or may not have something to do with finding your destined self. At a minimum it should not be at odds with your finding your destined self. If it does not get in the way of finding your piece of the puzzle, and you are getting what you want from it, you then must learn to be grateful for the work.

> Things give pleasure to life. People give meaning.
>
> S.N. 1949♀

As an elderly friend of mine said, "I cultivate an attitude of gratitude. When I saw that there were weeds in my garden that needed pulling, I felt grateful that I would be able to still bend over to pull them out."

To struggle against your job or the amount money you have is to struggle against the gifts the universe gives to become your intended self. If you struggle with either of these, you will not understand the nudge the universe is supplying. And, since we are all one in the puzzle, you are struggling not only against yourself but also against the intention of the whole.

What nudges are you getting from your job?

S.M.H 1949 ♀ ䷸

Notes to Self for Job

Want to work on the ideas in this chapter further? Deep Dive Exercises for Chapter Thirteen: Job are on Page 243.

Chapter 14

You are Unique in the Universe: Consider All Sources as You Look for Repeating Lessons

Once upon a time, a man named George lived next to a river. Since it was not uncommon for the river to flood in the spring, George was not surprised when he heard that the water was rising and due to crest higher than ever before. Nor was he surprised when he heard on the radio that he and everyone in his neighborhood should evacuate.

George had been though floods before. He figured he would ride it out at home, and being a religious person, he began to pray, "Lord, protect me from the flood."

As the water began to rise, there was a knock on his door.

"Time to evacuate, sir," said the policewoman. "Come with me now and I'll help you find shelter."

George declined her offer saying, "God will protect me from the flood."

The water continued to rise and soon began to fill the first floor of his house.

"Lord, protect me from the flood," he continued to pray as he was forced to move to the second floor.

As he looked out the second floor window at the rising water, a rescue boat floated by, and seeing him in the window, the coast guard captain driving the boat maneuvered over to the window.

"Climb into the boat, sir, said the captain. "Climb in and I'll bring you to safety."

George declined his offer saying, "God will protect me from the flood."

The floodwater continued to rise forcing George out onto the roof.

As he looked up from the roof, he saw a rescue helicopter in the distance. Seeing George on the roof, the pilot flew over, stopped on a neighboring roof and threw George a rope.

"Grab the rope and come over, sir," said the pilot. "I'll take you to safety."

George declined his offer saying, "God will protect me from the flood."

It was a record flood with the water level well over the roofs of most houses, and George drowned.

When George was entering the pearly gates, he asked God," Why didn't you save me?"

God replied, "I sent you a rescuer on foot, one in a boat and one in a helicopter. What more did you need?"

George was offered rescue three times, but since he was convinced his help would come in a specific manner, he didn't recognize all the rescue options given to him. His lack of open-mindedness cost him dearly.

S.M.H 1949 ♀ ䷀

The cooperative universe wants to support you on your journey to your destined self and will offer repeated nudges to get you there. It is persistent in its messaging; it uses many channels to get your attention. If you open yourself up to the cooperative universe, it will supply you with exactly what you need to grow on your journey. Frequently, these lessons come as new ideas and concepts, so each of us needs to be open to new ways of thinking as the cooperative universe gives us nudges and support. We need to be open to seeing things in new ways and learning new things in unanticipated ways. To be able to recognize repeating lessons, you need to look back at your journey, search for repeating messages and open yourself up to the variety of options the universe is supporting you — whether they fall within your learning style or not. You need to be open-minded and consider all sources. You need to get your mind ready to a rescuer in any form of helicopter.

> Cultivate options. You never know when you'll need an alternate path.
>
> J.C. 1965 ♂

The saying goes: if you do what you have always done, you will get what you have always gotten. To be able to reprogram your brain with new ways of thinking, you will need to begin to think differently. Once I believed that the universe was supporting me in unimagined ways, I looked not only at my tracks in the snow but also looked for *patterns* in my tracks in the snow. The cooperative universe presented me with ways of thinking and knowing that were uncomfortable. Looking back, when I suspended judgment and allowed my natural curiosity to lead me, new ideas always brought me to a place unimagined. One pattern repeatedly presented to me was astrology.

> Be grateful for and open to serendipity. Know when you have a challenge or opportunity that will impact your journey.
>
> J.S. 1946 ♂

While astrology may not be your rescuer, it was and is a powerful tool for me to transform to my destined self. Coupled with other lessons, astrology has had a profound impact on my thinking. It reinforced Personal Talking Point Number Two: *We are all on a journey, and we all have lessons to learn on this journey. If we open ourselves up, the cooperative universe always provides exactly what we need to learn, grow and discover the reason we are here.* And, it inspired my last two talking points:

Personal Talking Point Number Twelve: Each of us is born a unique being, and each of us is on a journey to claim our unique role on the world.

Personal Talking Point Number Thirteen: Lessons will be presented until they are learned.

It is not important whether you believe in the ideas presented in astrology; the tool is not important, but consider how each of the preceding three ideas reinforced a pattern for me.

Personal Talking Point Number Twelve: Each of us is born a unique being, and each of us is on a journey to claim our unique role on the world.

Astrology is the study of how forces emanating from celestial bodies influence human character. A person's natal astrological chart is a snapshot of where the planets and stars are at that precise moment at that precise location on earth.

> You are special and unique.
>
> V.O. 1920 ♀

This snapshot of a moment in time is ever changing, for the planets are always moving. This means no two charts can ever be alike. Each of the trillions of people who have lived, and who are living now, has a unique snapshot. Even twins have charts different from the other. Although perhaps only minutes apart, they are not born at precisely the same moment. Each twin has their own unique moment in time just as each person has their unique moment in time. Each of our births is a unique event in the universe. Your piece of the puzzle is also unique and vital to the puzzle. This idea alone makes me feel my life is important, makes me feel powerful, and compels me to find my piece of the puzzle.

Personal Talking Point Number Two: We are all on a journey, and we all have lessons to learn on this journey. If we open ourselves up, the cooperative universe always provides exactly what we need to learn, grow and discover the reason we are here.

I had already come to believe that difficult times in my life were teachers. Astrology reinforced this belief. The chart each of us received at birth provided us with all the gifts and challenges we need to learn, grow and discover our reason for being. Before each of us was born — somewhere in the ether — we worked with the cooperative universe to choose the map of our next path. I remind myself of this when I can't understand *why something is happening to me.* Before I was born, I chose it to move me along on this precise journey. The reason I want to learn the lessons presented in my chart is so I can move on to the next chart—the next life— a chart with new gifts and challenges. If my chart is chosen specifically for me, all of these choices provide me with the perfect journey. The purpose of the journey is to provide the tools for success during one life, so we can become our intended self and perform our piece of the puzzle and move to our next chart, our next incarnation.

> Only you are you and that makes you special.
>
> A.M.1926♂

Personal Talking Point Number Thirteen: Lessons will be presented until they are learned.

If you don't successfully complete the lessons presented on your path or if you don't successfully use your gifts to overcome your challenges, you will get another chance to try again in your next life. The lesson will be presented until it is learned. You will continue to receive nudges to find your piece of the puzzle. One chart leads to another. We are reincarnated from one life to the next.

Reincarnation is not contrary to conventional scientific thinking. Think of the law of conservation of matter that posits matter can neither be created nor destroyed, but only rearranged in another form. A tree that falls in the forest eventually decays to become forest nutrients. A log that is burned in a fireplace becomes ash. Is the essence of a person less likely than a tree to be recreated or destroyed? No matter what you call that essence — spirit, soul, core or heart — there is something never-ending in each person.

Personal Talking Points Number Two, Twelve and Thirteen exemplify how open mindedness can reinforce patterns the universe provides if we look for them. When I was in my 20s and wanting to meet new people in a new town, I signed up for an introductory astrology class at the local high school. This class was taught by a woman who had a strong Catholic faith and a strong belief in reincarnation informed by astrology. She also believed Jesus —and likewise Buddha—completed their last chart and moved to heaven or nirvana. They completed their journey on earth by completing all the lessons in the charts presented them. She was able to hold onto two seemingly different frames of reference, and so am I. Having been raised a Christian, I am comfortable calling this essence a soul because I find the idea of a soul consistent with rebirth though reincarnation.

The tenants of astrology confirm the power I have in my life and permit me to accept and be grateful for all parts of my journey and my life. My unique chart, determined at the precise location and precise moment of my birth, is a promise —a promise of unique gifts given to me—to address the unique challenges also given to me in my chart. Briefly, my chart indicated that while the first half of my life would be an uphill struggle, I would gain more prosperity and security as time goes on (Sun in fourth house). Communication was a gift given to me and was mentioned earlier as a *voice* (Mercury in Gemini). The placement of Jupiter in my chart lends strong support for my piece of the puzzle. Jupiter located in Aquarius means I was born to share spiritual activities designed to uplift humanity. My birth chart is a promise. A promise to help me fulfill my piece of the puzzle.

Your birth was also a promise, and this promise is what is celebrated on your birthday. When you have a birthday, begin to think of your uniqueness.

S.M.H 1949 ♀ ☱

In my soul, I know I have done this particular chart before. During my 60th year, I committed to not repeating it again. I committed to use my gifts to overcome my obstacles and move on to my next chart. With this understanding I knew with certainty I would find my puzzle piece during this lifetime —and I did.

> The world you know is the world you know. If you keep doing what you have always done your world and your view of that world will always stay the same.
>
> V.M. 1923 ♀

For you to consider all sources of information from the cooperative universe and uncover your intended self, you need to nurture certain qualities. You need to be willing to be:

- Creative in your thinking,
- Open-minded to new ways of thinking,
- Able to question your assumptions,
- Willing to change your thinking,
- Able to learn from past mistakes, and
- Alert to patterns in the wide array of ideas and experiences presented to you.

Here are some ideas of how can you prime the pump needed to do that:

- Engage in conversation with people who think differently from you and are out of your comfort zone.
- Engage people in meaningful conversation during your travels.

- Ask people to be on your personal board of directors who will challenge your thinking.
- Seek out books and research, paying particular attention to the ideas that were unanticipated and jar your thinking.
- Change your routine and you may think differently, have new insights and perhaps run across a new opportunity. Getting up earlier, calling an old friend or going to the bookstore to scan books may help.
- Be open to tools that you can not see, touch or feel. Tools like astrology, palmistry, Tarot, music or reading the bumps on your head. The tool is unimportant. Your openness to new tools is vital.
- Consider palmistry to help you see your unique path. One way to begin to explore palmistry is to look closely at several people's palms. Your palm is as unique as fingerprints and may show you important features about you and your destined self. Become curious about what makes you unique in the world and how that shows up in your palm.
- Revisit the ideas of the religion in which you were raised and find ideas that resonate with you now. For example, some Christians believe God has a plan for our lives. Proverbs 16:1 reads, "God makes no promises to do what we want but only to do what He wants and in a fashion that

pleases Him." Others believe just as nature has a plan for everything, there is a reason for each person to be a part of the larger scheme of things. For some, trusting your gut is an important part of establishing your understanding of why things happen as they do.

- Look for intersections of thought. Look for patterns. Compare them to your tracks in the snow. Interestingly, even St Augustine, who believed that God preordained who would be saved and who would be damned, also believed that each man has responsibility for his life, and while we have free will, God has foreseen how we will live.[xxi] Sounds very similar to the idea astrology presents: each of us has choices, but also has a path with lessons that will be presented until learned.
- Seek ideas that reinforce an affirmation you are saying.
- Are you being nudged in the direction by alternative thought? Might something you can not see, touch or feel be your helicopter?
- Consider using the affirmation: I am willing to risk the security of old ways for a fulfilling future.

So, if you believe in astrology —great. If you don't, try to substitute some other word or concept from your spiritual or religious understanding. God's plan for your life. The

> If we are destined to live our lives over and over again until we get it right, let me pass this on to you. Take it or leave it.
>
> K.A. 1951♀

way things are supposed to be. Find the frame to know you are unique and have a unique journey.

Whatever your vision of a higher power, know that it provides lessons for each of us. If you look for these lessons in your situation and your circumstances, you will begin to see all things — positive or otherwise — as opportunities to move along your journey.

The lesson will be presented until it is learned.

Think again of Ralph, whom I mentioned in the first chapter. Longing for the person he was meant to be, he dreamed that one day he would wake up and everything would be different. That had never happened, and he believed that he was too old to make his life different. Ralph will continue to get more opportunities from the universe to change his life, and if he doesn't get the lesson this chart, he will have another opportunity in the next.

Notes to Self for Chapter Fourteen

Want to work on the ideas in this chapter further? Deep Dive Exercises for Chapter Fourteen are on Page 248.

Chapter Fifteen

Reprogram Self-Sabotage: Road Blocks

I began drinking in high school because my friends did, and by college, I found I was more comfortable with drinkers than non-drinkers. While a little simplistic, my choice of sorority led me to the fun, drinking group rather than the more serious, studious group. Before pledge day, several people came to my dorm room to urge me to consider the more studious group. When I said I appreciated their request, I was going with the other, one girl said to me, "It is your decision, but I don't believe you belong with that group." My tracks in the snow now tell me she was right. My choice was a more far-reaching decision than I had ever imagined.

By my 50s I was drinking every day, but not getting drunk every day. I would have at least two glasses of wine each evening. As I looked at my tracks in snow, I saw I tried to quit many times, unsuccessfully.

When a friend had a 60th birthday party weekend at her north woods cabin, I performed a New Moon ritual. The New Moon is a time of beginnings and a time to set goals. Rituals are a way to mark turning points in your life, and they can symbolically welcome changes. The New Moon is a moment to conjure what seems out of reach, and creating the vision is the first step to making it a reality. I decided to use the New Moon to intentionally set the goal of quitting drinking.

Together with my friends, I made a fire outdoors, lit candles and held a few of my favorite agates from my collection in my hand. I lit a sage wand and cleared my mind with meditation and self-hypnosis. I wrote on a piece of paper that I intended to quit drinking by year's end. And, then I put the paper in the fire.

I felt I was on my way. This was reinforced by the fact the New Moon was also on my son's birthday a fact I found to be fortuitous. I created spreadsheets to mark the number of days without drinking.

By mid-December, I was still drinking. I was also preparing to go to the same friend's north woods cabin for the New Year as we always did. When I saw there was another New Moon, in Thomas Kuhn's terms, I think I felt the paradigm shift. I felt the branch break.

I met with my therapist and found I was surprisingly resistant to considering a treatment program. I finally agreed to an alcoholic assessment, but being the holiday season, the person I was referred to for the assessment didn't call me back right away.

With the New Moon pressing on my time clock, I turned to books, which have always been my friends, and rediscovered the previously mentioned book, Sober for Good,[xxii] by Anne Fletcher. Fletcher is a health journalist who interviewed over 200 people who had successfully quit drinking for more than five years. Each of them did it in their own unique way. The universe had provided just what I needed: permission to quit drinking in my own fashion.

A group of people staying at my friend's cabin went to a restaurant on New Year's Eve. I sat next to a man I had just met. When he ordered a non-alcoholic beer and I asked him why, we made a date to discuss it further during a walk the next day. His sharing during that walk reinforced the wisdom of quitting drinking in your own way and gave me permission to do just that.

On January 2, on another New Moon and on my daughter's birthday, I amended my intention to read — I quit drinking *instead of* I intend to quit drinking *— and I haven't had a drink since. The cooperative universe provided both the book and my new non-alcoholic beer drinking friend.*

By now, you have done or have begun to do the following. You have:

> Ask for help because it often is more fun to do things with others and the end product is better.
>
> **D.S. 1949♀**

- Accepted your invitation to the prom and know you can make the life changes you need to live your intended life,
- Begun thinking you are unique in this world and have confidence you were born at a unique time. You were born for a reason unlike anyone else's reason, and once you find that reason, you will find more peace and contentment in your life,
- Begun to look for your tracks in the snow; looking back on your life for patterns and clues for your unique puzzle piece,
- An understanding of the power of your thoughts and are beginning to monitor what you think,
- Written or adopted some affirmations and are crafting your own personal talking points,
- Begun to think about your board of directors,

- Come to believe that once you commit to transformation, you will receive support from all the forces of the universe,
- Thought about what your turning point is, was or could be,
- Come to believe that your journey —albeit not completely clear to you now — will result in your finding your piece of the puzzle, and
- An understanding of how to get other parts of the puzzle to support your journey.

You are well on your way to finding your destined self and your piece of the puzzle. But, unless you have no past and have lived in a vacuum most of your life, there are things that may get in the way of creating what you want in your life. Roadblocks on your journey.

Some may be new roadblocks, and some may be old. Some may have been thrust upon you, while others may have been unconsciously chosen. Some may be roadblocks you can remove yourself; others may need professional help to be removed.

> Fear kept me from driving a car. I wish I had worked through that fear and could drive now.
>
> C.L. 1930♀

One of the roadblocks requiring professional help is depression, and since this book is in no way a substitute for a skillful psychologist, depression is only addressed briefly here. I have been treated for clinical depression twice in my life. The first time, when I was no longer answering the phone and everything in my closet was too good for me to wear, a caring friend suggested I get help. I called, went in for a meeting with a psychiatrist and was promptly diagnosed with depression. I was encouraged. I figured if something was really wrong, it might be able to be fixed. Unfortunately, I couldn't get my next appointment for a month.

"What to do now that I know something is wrong?" I asked the doctor. "In general," he said, "It is better to be busy than not, and it is better to be with people than not."

Those words helped until I could get further help, and I share them with the hope they will help you, too. When I feel I am slipping into depression, I call a friend or get busy doing something. While I did not know about affirmations back then, if my younger self were slipping into depression, I would now suggest she use the following affirmations:

> The only things worse than being lonely, is wishing you were.
>
> D.B. 1952 ♂

- *I am grateful to say yes to all that I am and all this life has to offer.*
- *I am grateful to love and heal my body — every day in every way — and the universe reflects that back to me*
- *Every cell in my body is healthy and radiates health.*

If you have a problem with depression, seek professional help. If you are not sure if you need help, ask someone

> If being afraid of what might happen, changes what might happen – keep on being afraid.
>
> G.J. 1949 ♂

who knows you and whom you trust and then act accordingly.

> If you think the world has turned its back on you, look again.
>
> D.F. 1932♀

The roadblocks most within our control are those that we create ourselves.

Think of Joanie, the girl who was never invited to the prom. She was her own worst enemy.

Roadblocks of our own making are self-sabotage and stem from fear: fear of the unknown future and fear of success. Fear is a powerful emotion.

When I felt fearful about some future unknown event, I repeated my Personal Talking Point Number Eleven:

> Connect with the humor of life circumstances and laugh at yourself, and you will connect more fully with others.
>
> D.S. 1949♀

> Life is uncertain. Therefore, I will be flexible, resourceful and innovative. I will be proactive and smart but reading reality and knowing what is needed. I work on things that I can do something about and not focus on things that I can not control. I will be a part of the solution, not a part of the problem.

I also repeated the following affirmation:

> *I am a capable, competent person who can handle anything that comes my way, well.*

When I am fearful of unknown future failures, I remember failures on my journey that led to something unimagined and good. I actively look for the nudge in each "failure" and write them down, so I can find them when I can't remember their worth.

As you address your fears, remember two things. First, a problem is not a problem unless it has a solution. If it doesn't have a solution, it is a circumstance. Second, it is a problem if you think the problem is *out there,* because *out there* is not within your control. Two affirmations will help you keep this in mind:

> Find a way to get help when you need it.
>
> C.G. 1917 ♂

- *Every problem has a solution, and it is easy for me to find solutions to the problems I face.*
- *I am completely responsible for my reactions to all people, places and things.*

Distraction and avoidance are also forms of self-sabotage — things we do unconsciously to insure that we don't move along on our journey. If you are distracted from or avoiding your path, you will not find your piece of the puzzle.

There are many ways to be distracted and many ways to avoid the work you need to do. As noted in previous chapters, your job, money and other people can either help you find you piece of the puzzle or prevent you from doing so. All can be distractions. But we can choose to be focused. One reason that people unconsciously choose to distract or avoid what needs to be done on their journey is fear of success. You may fear that you *will* find your piece of the puzzle and have the ability to become your destined self. Why would someone fear such success? Does any of this sound familiar?

- Many people fear success because it tests their limits and opens the door to new situations that they fear they won't be able to master. In this way, success can expose weaknesses and demand that people deal with their flaws. A small voice in the back of your mind might be saying, "So, what if you do find your piece of the puzzle and you can't hack it?"

- The success of finding your destined self may involve change. With success may come more challenges and responsibilities. A small voice in the back of your mind may be saying," What if you can't measure up?"

- Sometimes people fear success because even though they have found their piece of the puzzle, they worry they won't live up to this achievement. They're afraid they don't have what it takes to rise to the challenge, and if they do, they fear they can't sustain it. A small voice in the back of your

> Name what scares you. Be specific. Then name what it takes to make that smaller. Then do that.
>
> H.M. 1957 ♂

mind may be saying, "You aren't good enough or smart enough to carry this off."

What are some clues that you are self-sabotaging?

> Obstacles are what you see when you take your eye off the goal.
>
> G.H. 1949 ♂

1. Are you distracted from doing what you have set in front of yourself as goals? This might be drinking too much, experimenting with drugs, staying out late so you are too tired to work towards your goal, being too busy at work, cleaning your house even when it doesn't need it, drinking so much coffee you can't sleep, believing that your are the only person to be able to help/straighten out your spouse/friend/child.
2. Do you put important things off for non-essential fluff or make-work? Others may perceive this as laziness. You may talk about your life dreams and goals all the time, but you watch TV every night and surf the web for hours every day. You never actually take practical steps or exert self-discipline to move in the direction of your goals.
3. Are you using negfirmations? Is that little voice saying, "I can't, so why try anyway?"

The payoff for these behaviors is you don't have to worry about succeeding. You have created and used an escape hatch, so you have an excuse for not doing well.

Remember Joanie and the prom? Remember Ralph thinking it was too late?

What did I do to stop sabotaging myself?

First, I realized I was self-sabotaging. One moment of clarity came when I began to experience the same problems in my second marriage that I did in the first. I was the only common denominator.

> Trust yourself.
> M.W. 1945 ♂

I then used the power of thought by repeating Personal Talking Point Number Four:

> People create and visualize their own reality. Knowing I am responsible for all my reactions to all persons, places and things, I choose my responses carefully, thus powerfully affecting my circumstance and helping to create my own reality. I know thinking the problem is "out there" is a problem.

Knowing that I was capable of change, I said the following affirmation:

> *I deserve all the good stuff the universe has in store for me.*

As I began to minimize distractions and put myself at the top of my to-do list, I discovered my primary manner of self-sabotage; the way I avoided finding my destined self: I covered the feelings of not being my destined self with alcohol. I could never have felt the branch breaking that would begin my transformation had I continued drinking.

Alcohol was a persistent problem for me. It was only as I looked at the tracks in the snow that I saw how alcohol had altered my course.

Quitting drinking was and continues to be much easier and much harder than I would have thought. When it is harder, I think of how my tracks in the snow veered with drinking, and I decide to keep my path under my control. I knew I could do it. So, I did — with the support of the cooperative universe.

> Don't run with that bunch of girls in high school. They'll introduce you to smoking, and you'll never get anything out of that.
>
> **D.E. 1925 ♀**

By this point in your reading, I hope you have found your cooperative universe. What the something is that is larger than you. What it is that makes you think of yourself as something special and enduring, that just happens to currently inhabit this body of yours. What it is that makes you a spiritual being. Your concept of this higher power will support what you discover, rid you of the things that distract you from reaching your goal and help you know you are unique.

If you are still struggling, begin to act as it you already know your something larger identity. A review of nearly

500 studies [xxiii] concluded that people who have a vision of spirituality have a higher level of well-being and self-esteem and lower levels of hypertension and depression.

It is the universe that wants you to find your place within it, and it is the universe that will support you in unimagined ways.

S.M.H 1949 ♀ ䷂

Notes to Self for Chapter Fifteen

Want to work on the ideas in this chapter further? Deep Dive Exercises for Chapter Fifteen are on Page 254.

Chapter Sixteen

The End of My Year and the Beginning of Yours

Over twenty-five years ago, I had a dream that I awoke in the night and began wandering around my house. Somehow, even though I was still in my house I managed to arrive at a room I had never been in before. I didn't know it even existed. This was both disorienting and disconcerting. As I acclimated to the dark room, I bumped into large objects. Feeling my way around them, I discovered they were furniture covered with sheets, covered the way one would cover things that were put in storage. In this dark room, it took me a long time to realize this was my furniture. And, suddenly, I remembered each piece. As I realized this, I realized how much I liked each piece. I examined each piece in the dark, enjoyed reac-

quainting myself with each one, but always covering up the piece again.

Using the dream metaphor, I have opened the blinds in the darkened room, uncovered the furniture and am enjoying the room. I have reclaimed the room that was always there waiting for me. In the same way by the end of my 60th year, I have reached the four goals I set for myself. I have reclaimed my life. At this moment as I write, I am mindful the end of my 60th transformational year is only one week away. It is a time for me to review and rejoice in my progress towards my goals. It is time to enjoy my room and the furniture in it.

Before I do, I want to emphasize I have come to see this transformation in the same way some scientists are now looking at the Big Bang theory. To refresh your memory, the Big Bang is the idea the universe has expanded from a primordial hot and dense condition (i.e. the beginning) at some finite time in the past (best guess about 13 billion years ago.) The material thrown off from this bang continues to expand to this day. I see my transformation as being similar in two ways. First, it emphasizes an important basis for my transformation —the fact we are all part of the same cooperative universe and have been for over 13 billion years. Second, just as even after 13 billion years the universe is still expanding, my journey to find my piece of the puzzle will not end with this year. It will go on. I will use this same strategy over time and intend to get better and better with implementation. I have started an upward spiral.

This led to my final personal talking point.

Personal Talking Number Fourteen: People are capable intentional self-transformation.

My decision to have a tattoo that symbolizes self-transformation — long before I knew what it would mean for me specifically — was the beginning and has had a ripple effect in my life.

In my 59th year, I intentionally committed to a transformation with four focus areas. I quit drinking alcohol, I got my finances under control, I let go of expectations I had of others and finally wrote this book.

Which of these will stay the same?

I can confidently say that I will not drink again nor will I ever let my finances be outside of my control again. The positive feeling surrounding both of these will continue to propel me.

And, while I also believe I will never go back to having the expectations of others I did previously, I know I will continue to understand what that means even more clearly. When I first considered this as one of the things on which I would focus during my transformation year, I thought about small things like my not expecting my family to empty the dishwasher. I now more clearly understand that expectations are resentments in the making, and I am becoming clearer on the breadth of expectations a person can have of another. So I no longer expect my loved ones to live their lives in a way that will keep me from worrying about them. It is their job to live their lives as best they can, and it is my job to be responsible for my reaction when I do worry about the direction their path is leading. Likewise, I no longer expect someone else to understand why I do what I do. For example, I welcomed and appreciated my friends' support while I was writing this book, but if they did not understand why I needed to write it, I controlled my response to their feelings and let go of my need to convince them.

If I think of my puzzle piece, I see this book as a part of a very vibrant and rich orange splotch that takes up nearly half of my piece. I believe that I was born to write this book because I was born to share the lessons from my journey with others on the journey to inspire them to greatness and give them a sense of optimism. So, while I will continue to try to get this book into the hands of those who need it, I will also be looking for more ways to share what I have

> Sometimes you have to be respectful enough of another person to keep your worries about them to your self.
>
> **B.C. 1967 ♂**

learned. I was born to share what I have learned, and I believe I have done so with those I known and loved throughout my life. But this book brought what I have learned into clear focus. It is my fervent wish to the cooperative universe that this book will allow me to help more people.

Kierkegaard is quoted as saying, "Be that self which one truly is." I started on a path to become who I truly am and on the way found a more authentic and joyful life. Once I started on this path — even though my first steps were small—I couldn't stop. I had begun an upward spiral, and it became a self-fulfilling prophecy.

I hope that you now believe we are all part of the same cooperative universe, and in this tight circle what one does impacts us all. I hope the proper placement of my piece of the puzzle allows you to find the correct placement of your piece. And your placement leads to another person's placement, and so on, and so on.

I want to note there were unintended consequences of my transformational year that can be summed up by saying I began to take better care of myself. Knowing that I was on a unique and important journey, I began to clear my mind and my surroundings of clutter. Knowing this body was the one that would help get me though this chart, I began to eat better (and less) food and began to exercise more. Knowing that all those who share this journey with me are part of the journey, I began to see the good in other people and wished them all well. I find I am less irritated these days. I find I am less discouraged. I find I am comfortable with this Susan.

It has been a good year for me.

Is it the beginning of your year?

Ask yourself. Have I experienced moments of clarity? Have I had a moment of clarity while reading this book? Have I had a nudge from the universe? Where are my nudges coming from?

People often grow up to be like their parents. In an interesting way, the philosopher, Socrates, wrote that his work was similar to his mother's work. She was a midwife. Socrates saw that his task in life, perhaps his piece of the puzzle, was to help people deliver. Just as a midwife does not have a baby but rather helps someone else give birth, so he saw his teachings as helping people "give birth" to insight that can only come from within that person. It can not be imparted by someone else.

The cooperative universe and I provide this book in an effort to support your finding the insight into the person you were intended to be. Only you can give birth to that person.

At the beginning of this book, I suggested that you put the date you began reading on the inside cover. It is up to you to decide what to do with this date. Could it be an anniversary to celebrate each year? If you began reading on the 10th of the month, could you put a tickler on your electronic calendar to keep you on track? You are the person with the most insight into your self. You decide what the date means to you. Be the expert on yourself.

I have one more visualization for you. Close your eyes and go to *your place*—your place of meditation and reflection.

Once you are relaxed, you begin walking. After a while you see a high school track and field area in the distance. You decide to walk over to see it on this beautiful sunny day. You find your way to the track and discover there is only one. You stand next to the track and feel the rush of air as the runner passes by you. The runner is smiling, enjoying the run.

When the runner passes by the second time, she motions to you to join her on the track. You again feel the rush of air as she goes by and notice the confident smile on her face.

When she is half way around the track, for some reason beyond your understanding, you get on the track and begin to run. Even though you are not sure why you are running or where this run will end, it feels good. It feels right.

Can you feel it?

As you round one of the bends in the track, you see the runner ahead is slowing down. You assume she wants to run with you, so you begin to run a little faster to catch up. When you are within a few yards of her, you see she has something in her hand. It is a baton. As you get closer, she looks back at you smiling and holds out her hand with the baton in it, offering it to you.

Can you see it?

The baton contains all the power and force of the cooperative universe.

Can you reach it? Do you grab it?

When you do, *your* year to find your puzzle piece will begin. Is this your year?

Notes to Self for Chapter Sixteen

Want to work on the ideas in this chapter further? Deep Dive Exercises for Chapter Sixteen are on Page 259.

Deep Dive Workbook

Each section of this workbook contains questions to prompt you to think about the content of each chapter and what it means for you. Honor how the book and workbook will best support your work. Begin where you want. Use this book or a journal for your work. Write often and freely as you find your piece of the puzzle.

Peace in the Puzzle: Becoming Your Intended Self

Chapter One: Deep Dive
The Puzzle, My Piece of the Puzzle and the Other Puzzle Pieces

Want to refresh your memory about this Chapter? Chapter One begins on Page 7.

The German poet, Johann Wolfgang von Goethe said:

> Until one is committed, there is hesitancy, the chance to draw back, always ineffectiveness. Concerning all acts of initiative and creation, there is one elementary truth, the ignorance of which kills countless ideas and splendid plans: that the moment one definitely commits oneself, then providence moves as well. All sorts of things occur to help one that would never otherwise have occurred. A whole stream of events issues from the decision, raising in one's favor all manner of unforeseen incidents and meetings and material assistance, which no man could have dreamed would have come his way. Whatever you do, or dream you can, begin it. Boldness has genius, power and magic in it. Begin it now.

Have you felt the tension between the life you are living and the life you are intended to live? Do you long for something more in your life? Have you ever felt yourself a part of something larger?

S.M.H 1949 ♀ ䷓

Imagine you are part of the jigsaw puzzle. Imagine that in this enormous puzzle, you are one unique piece. Imagine what the puzzle looks like without your piece; then imagine what it looks like with your piece in place. What do you feel?

In the story at the beginning of Chapter One, every year a farmer shares his seed corn with his neighbors to ensure that he has prize winning corn. What is your seed corn? Are you sharing it?

Peace in the Puzzle: Becoming Your Intended Self

Writing is a powerful tool. It focuses you in a way that nothing else can. You will be guided to write about your journey in this and following chapters. Write now about the way you want your life to be. Then write it again as though it were already the case.

If you have ever primed a pump, you know that it takes some water to get one that is dormant going. With just a little water and a little pumping, the water will flow freely. The tools in this book help you prime the pump. Do you trust that there is water below the surface? Are you ready to start pumping?

Chapter Two: Deep Dive

GPS: Tools for Your Journey

Want to refresh your memory about this Chapter? Chapter Two begins on Page 18.

Imagine yourself in a car at the beginning of a journey; the journey to your intended self. What is keeping you from driving? What do the dirty windshield, sun in your eyes and flashing dashboard light mean in your life?

Everyone has a to-do list. Where is finding your piece of the puzzle on your to-do list? Does it need to get on the list? Move up in priority?

Peace in the Puzzle: Becoming Your Intended Self

Chapter Three: Deep Dive
Advice from the Voices of Wisdom

Want to refresh your memory about this Chapter? Chapter Three begins on Page 23.

No matter what age you are . . . what advice would you give your younger self?

S.M.H 1949 ♀ 晶

Chapter Four: Deep Dive
Your Invitation to the Prom: What You'll Need to Attend

Want to refresh your memory about this Chapter? Chapter Four begins on Page 30.

What are your *what ifs* and *if onlys*?

How have you been a carrot, an egg or a coffee bean?

Deep Dive Workbook

217

Peace in the Puzzle: Becoming Your Intended Self

Chapter Five: Deep Dive

Looking Back: Your Tracks in the Snow

Want to refresh your memory about this Chapter? Chapter Five begins on Page 37.

What do the Voices of Wisdom tell us about discovering that one thing is?

> Accept who you are and don't take yourself so damn seriously! Focus on yourself, not what others have, say, do etc. As hokey as it may sound, follow your own feelings and what you know to be true. You don't have to follow a crowd to be happy. With love and (some) understanding from your older self.
>
> K.A. 1951 ♀

> Be authentic.
>
> T.L. 1965 ♀

> It is not what you have done that matters. It is what you have done with what you have learned that does.
>
> N.P. 1953 ♀

> Do not follow the crowd.
>
> L.E. 1954 ♀

What do you think of their ideas? How might they apply to you and your journey to find your piece of the puzzle?

What are your *tracks in the snow*? Are there patterns? Repeating messages? Are there forks in the road?

Do you know what your one thing is? Do you know what it isn't?

Peace in the Puzzle: Becoming Your Intended Self

Chapter Six: Deep Dive
The Power of Thought: Your Subconscious Mind

Want to refresh your memory about this Chapter? Chapter Six begins on Page 49.

Which of your thoughts and beliefs are you feeding? Any you'd like to stop feeding?

Close your eyes, relax and imagine one of your favorite spots. Is it a woodland scene? On the shore of the ocean? On a mountain top? Add colors, smells, quiet noises — whatever is needed to make you feel as if you are there. Continue to practice going to this place. With practice you can return there often. Describe your place here. Go to your place and consider what these voices of wisdom said:

S.M.H 1949 ♀

Make the most of what you have. Don't feel sorry for yourself. Don't tell people when you are having a bad day or feeling badly. Act as if you are having a good day and the bad day will pass.

D.H. 1922 ♀

Seeing a glass half full vs. half empty gets you a long way.

T.L. 1965 ♀

Never underestimate how much you are judged by how you look and what you wear. Don't forget to also wear a smile

T.L. 1965 ♀

Remember to appreciate EVERYTHING about yourself in this moment- how you looked, how you loved and were loved by others. Never let the critics tell you who you are. And be especially aware of the inner critic that robs you of the joy in today.

D.K. 1955 ♀

Deep Dive Workbook

Peace in the Puzzle: Becoming Your Intended Self

Chapter Seven: Deep Dive
The Power of Thought: Affirmations

Want to refresh your memory about this Chapter? Chapter Seven begins on Page 58.

Consider the affirmation

> *I am always in the right place, at the right time, and engaged in the right activity to become the person I was meant to be.*

What are you saying to yourself about this point in time? About right now? What do you need to say to help you find your puzzle piece? What affirmations do you choose?

S.M.H 1949 ♀ ䷁

What do you say to yourself frequently? Is it what you choose to continue to say? Is it helping you get what you want and where you want to go? Is there something a parent said to you when you were young that programmed you computer? If it was a negative affirmation, craft a positive one and begin to say it.

Peace in the Puzzle: Becoming Your Intended Self

Chapter Eight: Deep Dive
The Power of Thought: Personal Talking Points

Want to refresh your memory about this Chapter? Chapter Eight begins on Page 66.

Consider the following story:

Once upon a time a professor stood in from of his class with an empty mayonnaise jar, a box of two inch rocks, a box of pebbles and box of sand.

"Who can put all of these things into the jar?" asked the professor.

After some discussion, one student spoke for the others and said, "It can't be done, sir. Too much mass."

The professor picked up the box of rocks and gently placed them in the jar. He then picked up the box of pebbles and poured them into the jar, shaking it lightly. The pebbles rolled into the open areas between the rocks. The professor then picked up a box of sand and poured it into the jar. The sand filtered into all the extra space.

"This jar represents your life. The rocks are your value system, the building blocks of your life. The pebbles are the other things that matter, and the sand is the small stuff."

"If you put the sand or the pebbles into the jar first," he said, *"There is no room for the rocks. Set your priorities. Pay attention to the things that are critical to your happiness. Take care of the rocks first: the rest is just sand."*

Do you know what your rocks are?

What are your personal talking points? Are there things that you know for certain? Begin to note them here. As you consider, think again about giving advice to your younger self. Is what you would like to advise related to your talking points?

Peace in the Puzzle: Becoming Your Intended Self

Chapter Nine: Deep Dive
The Power of People Together We Are and Ocean

Want to refresh your memory about this Chapter? Chapter Nine begins on Page 81.

Deep Dive: Friends

What advice would you give your younger self about friends? What do you need to do to take that advice now?

Deep Dive: Family

What advice would you give to your younger self about family? What do you need to do to take your advice now?

Peace in the Puzzle: Becoming Your Intended Self

Deep Dive: Marriage and Partnerships

What advice would you give to your younger self about partnerships?
What do you need to do to act on the advice now?

S.M.H 1949 ♀ ䷓

Deep Dive: Overall Relationships

Humans are social beings, and we all have an innate desire for companionship. Scientists now believe that what really separates us from other primates is our sophisticated interaction with each other.[i] We can learn about the importance of human interaction from studies on its lack.[ii] Researchers are finding that people who feel lonely have higher blood pressure and weaker immune systems than those that are not. This research suggests that loneliness may even make the genes that promote inflammation more active.

Humans evolved by depending on one another, and at the core, the need to connect is as strong as the need to alleviate hunger, thirst and pain. At its most primal, those who fail to connect with others are more likely to die without passing on their genes; it is a matter of survival. So, while human interaction is sometimes a blessing and sometimes a curse, it is necessary to our well-being.

Consider the following advice to younger self and consider what advice you would give to your younger self about interaction with others. Then consider drafting some personal talking points in response.

> Stop using the words "I" and "me" so much and start using the using "we" more.
>
> I.N. 1920 ♀

> Talk less and listen more.
>
> E.B. 1934 ♀

> Always keep your word.
>
> T.L. 1965 ♀

Peace in the Puzzle: Becoming Your Intended Self

> Never take sides because life has no sides, everyone has their own glasses and mirrors. Listen to your heart more often than your mind. That will be difficult for you but you know it is your gift, don't feel shame because of it, people may not understand but they will know in their hearts. There is very little that is understandable about life's process except love. And that can only be known in the heart.
>
> A.L. 1948 ♀

> Confidence in one's self rubs off on those around you, helping everyone to live their best life.
>
> S.B. 1940 ♀

> You can be lonely in a crowd. Reach Out.
>
> J.C. 1968 ♂

> Learn what to do when you and another person don't want the same thing. Find middle ground.
>
> C.A. 1971 ♂

> You get to say NO. You don't have to do what you don't want to do, and you don't have to make excuses for it. Just plain NO is very empowering. And after people become familiar with your willingness to say it, they tend to respect you more.
>
> T.R. 1949 ♂

Chapter Ten: Deep Dive

Harness the Power of People: Your Personal Board of Directors

Want to refresh your memory about this Chapter? Chapter Ten begins on Page 109.

List five people that you would consider asking to be on your personal board of directors. What would you ask of them? If you are concerned about how your request will be received, imagine how you would react if someone asked this of you.

Peace in the Puzzle: Becoming Your Intended Self

Here is what our advisers wish they had known earlier about getting advice from others. What is your reaction to these ideas? If you agree with them, are you following the advice?

> Surround yourself with your own personal board of directors and maintain your network. Initiate relationships! It is who you know in business.
>
> C.C. 1956 ♂

> My current advice to anyone starting out in a career is simply — FIND A MENTOR!
>
> H.B. 1918 ♀

S.M.H 1949 ♀ ䷁

Chapter Eleven: Deep Dive

Snap: Four Steps to Self-Transformation

Want to refresh your memory about this Chapter? Chapter Eleven begins on Page 118.

Consider what our Voices of Wisdom said and think of them in regard to your turning points.

> Never take sides because life has no sides, everyone has their own glasses and mirrors. Listen to your heart more often that your mind. That will be difficult for you but you know it is your gift, don't feel shame because of it, people may not understand but they will know in their hearts. There is very little that is understandable about life's process except love. And that can only be known in the heart.
>
> **A.L. 1948♀**

> You have good ideas, thoughts and opinions. Stop saying what is safe and makes other people happy and stick with your real thoughts. Express yourself more often instead of keeping your opinions to yourself.
>
> **K.A. 1962♀**

> Choose your five most prominent strengths, then, every day for a week, apply one or more of these strengths in a new way. Strengths include things like the ability to find humor or summon enthusiasm, appreciation of beauty, curiosity and love of learning.
>
> **D.K.1915♀**

> Try to recognize the value of self-respect, the earlier the better. Better late than never, but still...
>
> **T.R. 1949♂**

Deep Dive Workbook

Peace in the Puzzle: Becoming Your Intended Self

What of this advice resonates with you? What advice would you give to your younger self about turning points?

Soren Kierkegaard said,

> There is nothing with which every man is so afraid as getting to know how enormously much he is capable of doing and becoming.

Are you ready to know how capable you are?

S.M.H 1949 ♀ 듦

Why is this a turning point in your life? Are you drowning? When do your swimming lessons begin?

Say the following affirmation several times out loud and write the thoughts that come to mind:

> *The turning point in my life has come I am open and receptive to living the life I love.*

Peace in the Puzzle: Becoming Your Intended Self

Chapter Twelve: Deep Dive

Get to *"just do it"*: Motivation

Want to refresh your memory about this Chapter? Chapter Twelve begins on Page 135.

Do you believe you can create the life you want to live? Why? What tools in this book can help you create that life?

S.M.H 1949 ♀ 冨

Do you want to do this the hard way or the easy way? What are you doing that makes it the hard way?

Peace in the Puzzle: Becoming Your Intended Self

Chapter Thirteen: Deep Dive

Harness Your Resources: Needs and Wants

Want to refresh your memory about this Chapter? Chapter Thirteen begins on Page

Deep Dive: Resources

Feeling prosperous? Do you remember a time when you felt prosperous? What would make you feel prosperous now?

Looking back, our advisers wished they would have known lots of things about money that they know now.

> More isn't always better. Sometimes less is more.
>
> J.C. 1965♂

> Tuck some money away from each paycheck.
>
> J.B. 1956♂

> Stop saying that I hope I win the lottery, and refuse to let your finances get out of control.
>
> T.P. 1947♂

> Save early and often.
>
> J.C. 1965♂

> Hoping your financial situation gets better without a plan won't get you out of debt.
>
> F.S. 1971♂

> Pay yourself first. Save at least 10% but 15 or 20% is even better. You'll be more comfortable during your retirement.
>
> M.T. 1955♀

> When money goes out the window, love goes out the door.
>
> J.M. 1916♂

> Understand in your youth the magic of compound interest. Save, save. Save.
>
> A.C. 1940♂

> Buy right to begin with. Don't stretch too far or sell yourself short.
>
> J.C. 1965♂

Peace in the Puzzle: Becoming Your Intended Self

Is money getting in the way of your finding your piece of the puzzle? What would you tell your younger self about money?

What do you need to do to be able to follow that advice NOW?

S.M.H 1949 ♀ ䷁

Finish these sentences

I am grateful in this moment for these seven places.

1. _____
2. _____
3. _____
4. _____
5. _____
6. _____
7. _____

I am grateful in this moment for these seven things.

1. _____
2. _____
3. _____
4. _____
5. _____
6. _____
7. _____

Deep Dive Workbook

Peace in the Puzzle: Becoming Your Intended Self

I am grateful in this moment for these seven people.

1. _____
2. _____
3. _____
4. _____
5. _____
6. _____
7. _____

Do you see a pattern of abundance? Does this pattern help you formulate any personal talking points?

Deep Dive: Job

Consider the following story as you think about what you want your job to do for you.

Once upon a time, a poor fisherman sat near the seashore under the shadow of a tree smoking his pipe. A rich man walked up to him and asked the fisherman why he was sitting under a tree smoking and not working.

The poor fisherman replied that he had caught enough fishes for the day.

Upon hearing this, the rich man got angry and said, "Why don't you catch more fish instead of sitting in shadow wasting time?"

The poor fisherman asked what he would do with more fish.

Patiently, the rich man replied, "You could catch more fish, sell them, earn more money and buy a bigger boat."

The poor fisherman asked what he would do then.

The rich man replied, "You could go fishing in deep waters and catch even more fish and earn even more money."

The poor fisherman asked what he would do then.

Peace in the Puzzle: Becoming Your Intended Self

The rich man said, "You could buy many boats and employ many people to work for you and earn even more money."

The poor fisherman asked what he would do then.

Proudly, the rich man said, "You could become a rich man like me."

The poor fisherman asked what he would do then.

Thinking that he had finally made his point the rich man said, "Don't you see you can become so rich you will never have to work for your living again! You can spend all the rest of your days sitting on this beach, looking at the sunset, smoking your pipe"

The fisherman smiled and said, "And what do you think I'm doing right now?"

What did the rich man want his job to do for him? What did the poor fisherman want his job to do for him?

S.M.H 1949 ♀ ䷀

What do you want your job to you for you? Does it do it? Are you grateful for it? Are changes needed? If so, what changes are within your control?

Consider what our advisers have to say about work:

> Don't let them convince you to retire. If you ever get a nice job, don't be so eager to quit your job. It might be hard to find another one, and you'll say, "I miss that job."
>
> D.E. 1927♀

> Don't burn bridges. So, they didn't give you the job, the raise whatever you wanted. Be gracious. You never know how or when your paths will cross in the future.
>
> D.L.1949♀

> Vigorous debate usually results in a better idea than a dictate from the boss.
>
> J.W. 1967♂

> It's not "Do what you love and the money will follow." It's "Do what you love...period." If the money comes, great. If not, hey, you're doing what you love! Work hard on figuring out what that is. Don't let yourself down by not doing that and allowing your so-called career to just happen. You run the risk that you'll have neither significant personal satisfaction nor huge financial rewards that would have at least helped.
>
> T.R. 1949♂

> Volunteering is the best reward you can give yourself.
>
> I.N. 1919♀

Deep Dive Workbook

Peace in the Puzzle: Becoming Your Intended Self

> My advice is simple. I offer two thoughts -- and wish you success as you "follow YOUR bliss" (ala my college professor Joseph Campbell)
>
> **H.B. 1918♀**

> If you are early in your career, don't assume you have nothing to offer. New brooms can sweep clean —or at least — cleaner.
>
> **M.C. 1950♀**

> Hard work was required in business in order for women to compete with men. Seems like that was a long time ago but in the mid seventies, it was expected that most women would not succeed as men did. So you worked harder and longer to make sure people understood what you could and did accomplish. As I succeeded, the long hours of work helped me accomplish much. I was able to progress into other positions, companies and in compensation. Yet that led to a pattern of long hours and less and less personal time. My advice to self is/was to create clearer boundaries for work and personal life. I always made time for the really important things but did not always make time for rest and personal pursuits. Not enough balance, I would say. Do I regret not having had enough personal time? This isn't so strong that I would say I have regrets. I never take that attitude in life. It isn't productive and isn't one that you can alter. So, no, I don't regret the work and life choices I made. However, if 30 years ago, I knew what I know now, I would have led to a more balanced lifestyle. Even if it meant not having the success I have had.
>
> **S.M. 1953♀**

> Don't burn bridges. So, they didn't give you the job, the raise whatever you wanted. Be gracious. You never know how or when your paths will cross in the future.
>
> **D.L. 1949 ♀**

> It helps to talk a good game, but performance is what matters most.
>
> **T.L. 1965♀**

> The first was written in my "autograph book," by my 4th grade teacher, Miss B. "Do well the little things now, and big things will come to you later asking to be done."
>
> **H.B. 1918♀**

What would you tell your younger self about work? What is preventing you from taking your advice now?

As you think about what advice you would give to your younger self about money and work, remember that it is a problem if you think the problem is out there because you can control the ones that you own. A problem without a solution is a circumstance. As you think about your advice to yourself, think about money and work as a part of your journey rather than something outside of you that causes problems. Be thinking of the affirmation —*I am completely responsible for all my reactions to all people places and things* —as you craft your advice to your younger self.

Peace in the Puzzle: Becoming Your Intended Self

Chapter Fourteen: Deep Dive

You are Unique in the Universe: Consider All Sources as Your Look for Repeating Lessons

Want to refresh your memory about this Chapter? Chapter Fourteen begins on Page

School isn't the only place we learn, and brain research tells us if we don't use it, we lose it, so it isn't surprising our advisers spoke to the importance of all kinds and manner of learning. Consider the words of the Voices of Wisdom below and how the ideas presented fit into your personal talking points.

> Keep your skills, abilities and achievements current. It's wonderful that you were the 6th grade spelling bee champ, but nobody really cares except your mother. Don't rest on your laurels.
>
> T.L.1965♀

> Read. Grow. Do crossword puzzles. Take advantage of every opportunity to learn. And try to distinguish between what matters and what doesn't.
>
> T.R. 1949♂

> Be curious and get second opinions from bankers, lawyers, auto mechanics and real estate agents.
>
> K.K.1925♂

> Learning is important! Celebrate the learning already achieved and the tragedies avoided and enjoy learning more every day.
>
> N.W. 1922♂

> Stay in school —discipline yourself!
>
> P.R. 1952♀

> Keep your curiosity. Wonder about everything. Speak up. You've got a right to your opinion just like anyone else. And don't forget to listen — you may change your opinion based on another person's vision.
>
> S.A.1946♀

In all things —be humble. The older you get, the more you realize that you know very little.

J.C.1965♂

Learn something new everyday.

T.M. 1938♂

Don't give up the piano.

C.R.1950♀

Read everything you can. Not just novels, but non-fiction that helps you see another's view point. Everyone goes though life differently and it is good to understand how other people think and feel.

D.H. 1922♀

Study harder.

R.H. 1929♂

When I was one month from graduating from high school, our barn burned to the ground. Instead of going to school, I became a nanny. I would tell my younger self... continue your education! In the long run, it is more expensive not to.

B.M. 1920♀

When you are in college, take advantage of what the school has to offer – all of what it has to offer. Think about your decision to not take a foreign language. You might need it someday.

C.R. 1919♂

Peace in the Puzzle: Becoming Your Intended Self

Open yourself up to new learning and new thinking. Actively seek them out. Do so consciously and consider the words of Henry David Thoreau:

> I know of no more encouraging fact than the unquestionable ability of man to elevate his life by conscious endeavor.

What new ways of learning and thinking interest you? What alternate ways of thinking have you already explored or been drawn to?

What would you tell your younger self about learning? What do you like to learn? What interests you? What part of the newspaper do you read first? What type of books do you like to read? What topics do you consistently seek out? What tracks in the snow can you discover from your school days?

Peace in the Puzzle: Becoming Your Intended Self

Consider the following:

> Perhaps there is a pattern set up in the heavens for one who desires to see it, and having seen it, to find one in himself.
>
> **Plato**

> Destiny grants us our wishes, but in its own way, in order to give us something beyond our wishes.
>
> **Johann Wolfgang von Goethe**

How might the ideas of reincarnation and astrology fit into your religious or spiritual framework? If the word "astrology" has bad connotations for you, suspend judgment and consider what many prominent people have said about it:

- President Theodore Roosevelt kept his horoscope in the oval office and is attributed to saying, "I always keep my weather eye on the opposition of my seventh house Moon to my first house Mars."

- J. P. Morgan, America's first billionaire, said, "Millionaires don't use astrology, billionaires do."

- Physicist Albert Einstein said, "Astrology is a science in itself and contains an illuminating body of knowledge. It taught me many things and I am greatly indebted to it."

- Mark Twain said, "I was born with Halley's Comet and I expect to die upon its return," and he did.

- Carl Jung, one of the founding fathers of psychology said, "Astrology is assured recognition from psychology without further restrictions, because astrology represents the summation of all the knowledge of antiquity. The fact that it is possible to construct, in adequate fashion, a person's character from the data of his nativity shows the validity of astrology."

Can you see patterns and intersections of thought in your life? What are they? What is the message the universe is giving you?

Peace in the Puzzle: Becoming Your Intended Self

Chapter Fifteen: Deep Dive

Reprogram Self-Sabotage: Road Blocks

Want to refresh your memory about this Chapter? Chapter Fifteen begins on Page 188

You are reading this book because you want something more, but are you self sabotaging? Are distractions getting in the way of you finding your authentic self? What are they? If it is a problem, then it has a solution. What would your older self tell you?

Are you avoiding becoming your destined self? What do you use to avoid? What would your older self tell you?

Close your eyes and visualize the universe providing what you need to reach the goal you have set. Some people see a kindly man with a gray beard on the throne. Some see warm light radiating on them and on their path. What does it look like to you?

Peace in the Puzzle: Becoming Your Intended Self

Consider this story:

Once upon a time a man was walking in the woods, when he heard a young child reciting the alphabet.

He stopped and asked the child, "What are you doing? Practicing your ABCs?"

The boy looked him in the eye and said, "No, I am praying. I don't know the word, so I figure God can use this to spell them out."

Visualize this force and ask for what you need to accomplish your goal. Don't be concrete about what you are asking. You can connect and merely say your ABCs.

Consider the words of the Voices of Wisdom:

> Know that not everything is your fault.
>
> S.J. 1949♀

> When you fear failure, think what your older self would tell you... then go for it.
>
> B.W. 1919♀

> You get to say NO. You don't have to do what you don't want to do, and you don't have to make excuses for it. Just plain NO is very empowering. And after people become familiar with your willingness to say it, they tend to respect you more.
>
> T.R. 1949♂

> Ask for help when you need it. You don't have to know everything.
>
> K.R. 1954♀

> You are happier when you are DOING things. Stop thinking so much about what might happen if you do/don't do a particular thing and just DO the things you want to do.
>
> K.A. 1962♀

> Forgive yourself for being young and foolish when you were young and foolish.
>
> B.W. 1919♀

> Remember that day when everything in your closet was too good for you to wear? If that happens again, don't wait to get some help with depression.
>
> J.G. 1935♀

Is depression getting in the way of your finding your authentic self? If it is a problem, then it has a solution. What would your older self tell you?

Peace in the Puzzle: Becoming Your Intended Self

Think about the answers your older self would give your younger self if asked the following questions:

- When do I feel fully alive?
- When have I felt the spirit of life?

Close your eyes and imagine those times. Choose one of them and take yourself there mentally. If you are feeling depressed, it is better to be active than inactive and with people rather than alone. What are you doing today to be more active and engaged?

Chapter Sixteen: Deep Dive

The End of My Year and the Beginning of Yours

Want to refresh your memory about this Chapter? Chapter Sixteen begins on Page 202

A stone sculptor hits the stone many times before it cracks. It is not the last hit that created the crack but all the hits leading up to it. If this is your year, how will you remember this story and honor your process and the time it will take?

Mark your calendar for one week from today with this question: Am I still hitting my rock?

Peace in the Puzzle: Becoming Your Intended Self

Once upon a time a hunter shot down a wild goose. Since he was only wounded in one wing, he was able to land safely in a barnyard filled with turkeys and chickens.

At first, the turkeys and chickens were quite startled by this sudden visitor from the sky, but soon they became more comfortable with this stranger. They were able to ask the question that all non-flying birds ask of flying birds, "What is it like to fly?"

"It's wonderful!" said the goose, "It's beautiful to soar out in the wild blue yonder!"

The goose missed flying, so continued to tell more stories of flight. He told how a barn looks only an inch high from the air, and each animal and person looks like a tiny specks. He told of flying through clouds and feeling the wind on his face.

All the birds loved the goose's stories, and soon it became a weekly event for the goose to entertain all the barnyard birds with his stories. They even provided a little box where he could stand so everyone could see him better.

But while the domestic birds loved hearing about the glories of flight, they never tried to fly themselves. And the goose, even though his wing healed, continued to talk about flying but never actually flew again.

S.M.H 1949 ♀ 킄

Reading about transformation is not transforming. Dreaming of finding your destined self is not finding your destined self.

What do you need to do to more beyond reading and dreaming?

Are you merely managing change or creating future through change?
Remember — the best way to predict future is to invent it

Deep Dive Workbook

Appendix

1. *Personal Talking Points*
2. *Affirmations*
3. *Your Personal Talking Points*
4. *Your Advice to Your Younger Self*
5. *Your Tracks in the Snow*
6. *Parking Lot*
7. *References*

I. Personal Talking Points

A woman came to a wise man and asked for help; she asked him to tell her son to give up eating sugar. The wise man said he would help as he could and told the woman to bring the boy back in a week. Exactly one week later the woman returned, and the wise man said to the boy, "Please give up eating sugar."

The woman thanked him, but as she turned to go, asked him why he had not said those words a week ago.

The wise man replied, "Because a week ago, I had not given up eating sugar."

My personal talking points are things that I know with certainty are true for me. As with the wise man, I can recommend that you craft your personal talking points and use them often, because I use them myself.

1. The only things I truly own and control are contained in my brain. I will therefore learn as much as I can and guard against putting garbage in.

2. We are all on a journey, and we all have lessons to learn on this journey. If we open ourselves up, the cooperative universe always provides exactly what we need to learn, grow and discover the reason we are here.

3. The universe constantly provides opportunities for growth; therefore, I am open to them. Difficult circumstances often create paradigm shifts, whole new frames of reference by which people see themselves, the world, others in the world and what life is asking of them. I will therefore not fear difficult circumstances because of the opportunity they bring.

4. People create and visualize their own reality. Knowing I am responsible for all my reactions to all persons, places and things, I choose my responses carefully, thus powerfully affecting my circumstance and helping to create my own reality. I know thinking the problem is "out there" is a problem.

5. People believe what you tell them. One good story is worth more than any amount of research.

6. Everything in this world is influenced by people. I will therefore, treat all people with respect and tolerance. What goes around comes around.

7. People are capable of change, but people will only do things that are important to them. Being important to me doesn't make them important to someone else.

8. A person can create a vision of another person that impacts how they perceive themselves. Therefore, I will be a light, not a judge and a model, not a critic. I will surround myself with people who value me and make my perceptions more accurate.

9. People can have secondary greatness or social recognition, and not have primary greatness, or goodness in their character. Therefore, I will remember that being is more important than having.

10. There is more than enough good stuff to go around; therefore, I will delight the success of others as well as my own.

11. Life is uncertain. Therefore, I will be flexible, resourceful and innovative. I will be proactive and smart by reading reality and knowing what is needed. I work on things that I can do something about and not focus on things that I can not control. I will be a part of the solution, not a part of the problem.

12. Each of us is born a unique being, and each of us is on a journey to claim our unique role on the world.

13. Lessons will be presented until they are learned.

14. People are capable of intentional self-transformation.

II. Affirmations

Below are all the affirmations referred to in this book and many more that may become your favorite. Please remember that affirmations are powerful and for an affirmation to be effective it needs to be in the present tense, it must have a positive message, and it must be specific to your needs and personalized.

- *I am a capable, competent person who can handle everything that comes my way well.*

- *I am always in the right place, at the right time, engaged in the right activity to become the person I was meant to be.*

- *Every day in every way, I'm getting better and better.*

- *It is easy for me to be grateful for who I am and the life I live.*

- *I am grateful to life for all that I have received until now and for all that I will be receiving in the future.*

- *All is well. Everything that is happening is only for the highest good of me.*

- *I am completely responsible for all my reactions to all people, places and things.*

- *All my relationships are long lasting and loving.*

- *In life, I always get what I give out and I always give out love.*

- *I deserve love and I get it in abundance.*

- *People are good. The best is yet to come.*

- *I follow the principle of live and let live.*

- *I have compassion and kindness for all.*

- *It is easy for me to allow others to move successfully though their journey just as I move though mine.*

- *I trust my loved one has the support of the cooperative universe just as I do.*

- *The turning point in my life has come. I am open and receptive to living the life I love.*

- *It is easy for me to allow others to move successfully though their journey just as I move though mine,*

- *I trust that my loved one has the support of the cooperative universe just as I do.*

- *My goal is enjoy the journey to claim my piece of the puzzle. I know once I claim it, I will claim my peace in the puzzle.*

- *Everything I need I already have.*

- *I am a beloved child of the cooperative universe and (by writing this book), I am claiming my piece of the puzzle.*

- *I am grateful to say yes to all that I am and all this life has to offer.*

- *I am grateful to fully realize that I deserve what I desire.*

- *I have the ability to elevate my life by conscious endeavor; I know what those endeavors are and can easily and successfully perform them*

- *I have more than enough money to do all the things I want and need to do.*

- *Money is good, and I enjoy having money.*

- *Money flows into my life easily.*

- *Everyday my bank balance is more than that of the previous day.*

- *I am a money magnet and attract money continuously.*

- *I am getting more and more prosperous day by day.*

- *I enjoy having abundance in my life.*

- *Every problem has a solution, and it is easy for me to find solutions to the problems I face.*

- *I am grateful to say yes to all that I am and all this life has to offer.*

- *I am grateful to love and heal my body — every day in every way — and the universe reflects that back to me*

- *Every cell in my body is healthy and radiates health.*

- *I deserve all the good stuff the universe has in store for me.*

- *I enjoy life's challenges, and I learn from everything that happens in my life.*

- *I live each day with passion and power.*

- *I have tremendous confidence in my talents and my abilities.*

- *I have deep respect for myself and for everyone I meet each day.*

- *I forgive myself and others easily.*

- *I am willing to risk the security of old ways for a fulfilling future.*

- *I am aware of the priceless value of my life and the life of everyone I meet.*

- *I am always at peace because I trust and follow my internal guidance.*

Your own affirmations.

- _____
- _____
- _____
- _____
- _____
- _____
- _____
- _____
- _____
- _____
- _____
- _____

III. Your Personal Talking Points

Personal talking points are things that I know for sure, and they can be used when just about any question comes up to reinforce positive self-talk and support affirmations. Begin to craft your personal talking points.

IV. *Your Advice to Your Younger Self*

Here is what to do to give your advice in the form of a letter to your younger self:

- Pick a point in time when you were younger. You may pick the day you graduated, the day you got your first job, the day your heart was broken for the first time, or you may just want to divide your current age by two.

- Write a letter to your younger self and provide the best advice you can give. This is your letter, and there are no rules, but to help your thinking, the letter could give advice as business-like as "plastics" ala 1970's movie with Dustin Hoffman, The Graduate, as practical as "only floss the teeth you want to keep," as meaningful as "have confidence in your intuition," as spiritual as "open yourself up to the universe and the universe will provide every thing you need" or a combination of all of these. What do you wish you would have known?

V. Your Tracks in the Snow

The universe wants each of us to find our piece of the puzzle and supports us in so doing. Use 20/20 hindsight to turn around and see where your tracks in the snow have led you. Look for patterns, repeating tracks and forks in the road.

VI. *Parking Lot*

Sometimes ideas fit into a pattern and sometimes they don't. Use this space to park ideas that are important to finding your piece of the puzzle but don't fit just yet.

Peace in the Puzzle: Becoming Your Intended Self

VII. References

---

[i] Pratt, Laura A & Brody, Debra J. (2008, Sept) Depression in the United States Household Population, 2005-2006. NCHS Data Brief No. 7 ttp://www.cdc.gov/nchs/data/databriefs/db07.pdf

[ii] Manly, R. (2007, January) Go Ahead and Smile. Inside CLUSB. 59, http://www.csulb.edu/misc/inside/archives/v59n1/1.htm

[iii] Radhakrishnan, S. (1940). Eastern religions and western thought. Oxford: Oxford Univ. Press.

[iv] Dhammapada,. Dharmatrata., & Rockhill, W.W. Udanavarga: A collection of verses from the Buddhist canon. 5:18 S.l.: Oriental Pr.

[v] Leviticus 19:18

[vi] Shast-na-shayast 13:29

[vii] Confucius. The Analects 15:23 Gardners Books.

[viii] Haksar, A.N.D. (1998) The Hitopadesa. New Delhi: Penguin Books. Matthew 7:12

[ix] Matthew 7:12

[x] "John T. Bullitt", edited by John T. Bullitt. Access to Insight, 8 June 2010, http://www.accesstoinsight.org/lib/authors/bullitt/index.html.

[xi] Campbell, Joseph, Moyers, Bill D., & Flowers, Betty S. (2008). The Power of Myth. Paw Prints.

[xii] Kuhn, Thomas S. (1970) The Structure of Scientific Revolutions, Second Edition,. Chicago: University of Chicago Press.

[xiii] Swami Vivekenanda.(1956) Raja-Yoga. Copyright by Swami Nikhilananda. Trustee of the Estate of Swami Vivekenanada. Aristotle. Essay on the nature of ethics.

[xiv] Aristotle. Essay on the nature of ethics.

[xv] Maslow, A (1954) Motivation and personality. New York: Harper and Row.

[xvi] IBID

[xvii] Kierkegaard, S., Hong, E. H., Hong, H. V., & Hong, H. V. (1983). 6*Fear and trembling. Repetition. Princeton, N.J: Princeton Univ. Pr.

[xviii] Fletcher, A. (2003) Thin for Life: 10 Keys to Success from People Who Have Lost Weight and Kept It Off. New York: Houghton Mifflin Harcourt.

[xix] Fletcher, A. (2002) Sober for Good: New Solutions for Drinking Problems--Advice from Those Who Have Succeeded. New York: Houghton Mifflin Harcourt.

[xx] Seligman, M. (2002). Authentic Happiness: Using the New Positive Psychology to Realize Your Potential for Lasting Fulfillment. New York: Simon and Schuster.

[xxi] Augustine. & Williams, T. (1993). On free choice of the will. Indianapolis: Hackett

[xxii] Fletcher, A. (2002) Sober for Good: New Solutions for Drinking Problems--Advice from Those Who Have Succeeded. New York: Houghton Mifflin Harcourt.

[xxiii] Yeung, W. J & Chan, Y. (2007). The positive effects of religiousness on mental health in physically vulnerable populations: A review on recent empirical studies and related theories. International Journal of Psychosocial Rehabilitation. 11 (2), 37-52

www.ingramcontent.com/pod-product-compliance
Lightning Source LLC
Chambersburg PA
CBHW080333170426
43194CB00014B/2542